The Founding Fathers: A Very Short Introduction

VERY SHORT INTRODUCTIONS are for anyone wanting a stimulating and accessible way into a new subject. They are written by experts and have been translated into more than 40 different languages.

The series began in 1995 and now covers a wide variety of topics in every discipline. The VSI library now contains more than 400 volumes—a Very Short Introduction to everything from Indian philosophy to psychology and American History—and continues to grow in every subject area.

## Very Short Introductions available now:

Available soon:

MEDIEVAL PHILOSOPHY
    John Marenbon
SLANG  Jonathon Green

EARTH SYSTEM SCIENCE  Tim Lenton
THE WELFARE STATE  David Garland
CRYSTALLOGRAPHY  A. M. Glazer

For more information visit our website

www.oup.com/vsi/

R. B. Bernstein

# THE FOUNDING FATHERS

A Very Short Introduction

OXFORD
UNIVERSITY PRESS

# OXFORD
UNIVERSITY PRESS

Oxford University Press is a department of the
University of Oxford. It furthers the University's objective
of excellence in research, scholarship, and education
by publishing worldwide.

Oxford   New York
Auckland   Cape Town   Dar es Salaam   Hong Kong   Karachi
Kuala Lumpur   Madrid   Melbourne   Mexico City   Nairobi
New Delhi   Shanghai   Taipei   Toronto

With offices in
Argentina   Austria   Brazil   Chile   Czech Republic   France   Greece
Guatemala   Hungary   Italy   Japan   Poland   Portugal   Singapore
South Korea   Switzerland   Thailand   Turkey   Ukraine   Vietnam

Oxford is a registered trade mark of Oxford University Press
in the UK and certain other countries.

Published in the United States of America by
Oxford University Press
198 Madison Avenue, New York, NY 10016

© Oxford University Press 2015

Library of Congress Cataloging-in-Publication Data
Bernstein, Richard B., 1956–
The founding fathers: a very short introduction/
R. B. Bernstein.
pages   cm.—(Very short introductions)
ISBN 978-0-19-027351-4 (pbk.: alk. paper)
1. Founding Fathers of the United States—Biography.
2. United States—History—Revolution, 1775–1783—Biography.
3. United States—History—1783–1815.   I. Title.
E302.5.B46   2015
973.3092'2—dc23 [B]     2015010705

Printed by Integrated Books International, United States of America
on acid-free paper

*I dedicate this book to my students and colleagues at my new academic home, City College of New York's Colin Powell School for Civic and Global Leadership and its Skadden, Arps Honors Program in Legal Studies. This is a wondrous place to teach, learn, write, and work, and I am profoundly grateful to be here.*

# Contents

# List of illustrations

# Preface

In this short book, I propose to brush aside prevailing caricatures of the founding fathers and to offer general readers a distilled introduction to the subject, synthesizing the remarkable work that so many of my colleagues have produced. Chapter 1 explores the words, images, and meanings that we associate with the founding fathers, clearing the ground for the substantive inquiry the rest of this book presents. Chapter 2 sketches three contexts—geographical, political, and intellectual—that shaped the founding fathers. Chapter 3 explores the array of challenges that the founding fathers faced, meeting most but not all of them and leaving others for future generations to solve. Taken together, those challenges met and those challenges shirked define the founding fathers' creation of the United States and its constitutional and political systems. Chapter 4 traces the ways that posterity has sought to understand the founding fathers and has come to terms with their labors and their ambiguous legacies. The Epilogue uses the words of five great African American orators to explore the concept of perfecting the Union, as a way to answer enduring questions about our thorny and conflicted relationship with the founding fathers and their legacies.

This book takes the founding fathers down from their pedestals without knocking them down. At the same time, it sets their achievements and their failures within the context of their own time and place, while making clear that those achievements were not great beyond the bounds of mortal men and that those failures were not blameworthy beyond human beings' normal capacity to err. If we meet the founding fathers eye to eye instead of gazing reverently upward or sneering contemptuously downward, perhaps we can form a more pragmatic sense of who they were, what they did and failed to do, and why we care.

# Acknowledgments

It is gratifying beyond measure to join the Very Short Introduction series. Yet again, I am grateful to those who have helped me along the way. I absolve them from any mistakes, errors of judgment, and wackosity remaining in these pages.

My first debts are to my family, who has stood by me with this book as with all my earlier books. I also remember my mentors: Henry Steele Commager (1902–1998) and Richard B. Morris (1904–1989).

Nancy E. Toff, my peerless editor at Oxford University Press, continues to muster exemplary patience, faith, encouragement, and goading in dealing with me. Many thanks also to her colleagues at Oxford—senior production editor Joellyn Ausanka; copy editor Patterson Lamb; and their colleagues.

I am yet again indebted to the New York University Legal History Colloquium, a group founded by Professor William E. Nelson of New York University School of Law in 1981 and presided over by him ever since. Professor John Phillip Reid inspired in his own unique way (including his discovery of the important unpublished manuscript by Franklin Pierce in which Pierce insisted on the importance of New Hampshire to the American founding).

Professor Joanne B. Freeman of Yale University and I have been talking and writing about the "founding guys" for longer than either of us will willingly admit; she has taught me far more about history and the founding guys than I can recount. Joanne's mentor, Peter S. Onuf, newly retired as the Thomas Jefferson Foundation Professor of History at the University of Virginia, continues to be "mentor from heaven" (Joanne's phrase) to us all. Professor Charles L. Zelden of Nova Southeastern University, my scholarly brother, continues to have more faith in me and in my work than I do. His sage counsel and his collegial friendship are indispensable to me. That is true, as well, of other faithful friends, including Professor Carla Spivack of Oklahoma City University Law School; Professor Felice Batlan of Chicago-Kent Law School; Professor Annette Gordon-Reed of the Harvard Law School; Dr. Gaspare J. Saladino of the *Documentary History of the Ratification of the Constitution and the Bill of Rights* and his colleagues John P. Kaminski, Richard Leffler, and Charles Schoenleber; the redoubtable team guiding the *Documentary History of the First Federal Congress*: Charlene Bangs Bickford, Kenneth Russell Bowling, Helen E. Veit, and Charles DiGiacomantonio; Dr. Maeva Marcus of the Institute for Constitutional History at New-York Historical Society and George Washington University; Professor emeritus George Athan Billias of Clark University and his wife, Margaret, Julie Silverbrook of ConSource, and many others in the community of historians and other scholars who make study of the founding guys so rewarding.

My friends, the "usual suspects" in my life, have never stinted in insight, encouragement, and patience: Phillip A. Haultcoeur; Maralyn Lowenheim; Maureen K. Phillips and Joseph Newpol; Mark Gaston; the documentarians *extraordinaire* Ron Blumer and Muffie Meyer; April Holder and Michelle Waites; Kevin Griffin and Elissa Wynn; Edward D. Young III, his wife, Gina Tillman-Young, and their children, Christa, Adam, Noah, Luke, Mary Maya, Peter, and Moses; Molly Myers and Hasan Rizvi and their sons, Zane and Jehan; and Internet friends Karen Spisak,

Natalie D. Brown, Patrick Feigenbaum, Marion Pavan, Robert K. Folkner, Philip Whitford, Cynthia E. Nowak, and Kevin J. Hutchison.

Three friends did not live to see this book. First is the late, great Pauline Maier of MIT (1938-2013), one of the finest scholars whom I have ever known, and a cherished friend who always has been an example to me. Second is the late Marilee B. Huntoon (1955-2011), the best friend I've ever had. Third is Boo Freeman (2000-2014), the world's best bird, loyal cockatiel to Joanne B. Freeman. Boo taught me that animal companions have strong, clear, and winning personalities, and great depths of heart and loyalty. (I miss you, Boo.) Their memories always will be blessings to all who knew them.

Clark's Restaurant in Brooklyn Heights was a nursery for this book and a refuge for its author.

# Chapter 1
# Words, images, meanings

Because the phrase "founding fathers" is central to how Americans talk about politics, we might assume that it has a long history. And yet, for an expression that has become central to understanding the American past, "founding fathers" has a short life. It was first coined in the early twentieth century, and its inventor is no one you might expect.

On June 7, 1916, Senator Warren G. Harding of Ohio delivered the keynote address at the Republican National Convention. Harding looked like a statesman—tall and commanding, with silver hair, dark eyebrows, and olive skin. Now he intoned, "We ought to be as genuinely American today as when the founding fathers flung their immortal defiance in the face of Old World oppressions and dedicated a new republic to liberty and justice."

Harding's speech is the first recorded appearance of the phrase "founding fathers"—but he had come close four years before. On June 22, 1912, at the Republican National Convention, he nominated President William Howard Taft for a second term. Facing a divided and contentious audience (split between backers of Taft and supporters of Theodore Roosevelt), Harding proclaimed, "Human rights and their defense are as old as civilization; but, more important to us, the founding American

1

1. Coiner of the phrase "founding fathers," President Warren G. Harding also warned Americans not to regard their historical heroes as supermen.

fathers wrote the covenant of a people's rule into the bond of national life, beyond all erasure or abridgment."

Over the next five years, Harding recycled "founding fathers." On February 22, 1918, as featured speaker at a Washington's Birthday commemoration hosted by the Sons and Daughters of the American Revolution, he declared: "It is good to meet and drink at the fountain of wisdom inherited from the founding fathers of the Republic." Then, in 1920, after party leaders at the Republican convention chose him as their presidential nominee, Harding invoked the "founding fathers" in his acceptance speech. Finally, on March 4, 1921, President Harding said in his inaugural address: "Standing in this presence, mindful of the solemnity of this occasion, feeling the emotions which no one may know until he senses the great weight of responsibility for himself, I must utter my belief in the divine inspiration of the founding fathers.

Surely there must have been God's intent in the making of this new-world Republic."

Harding's creation passed into popular use swiftly and easily. Not until the 1960s, when the Library of Congress's Congressional Research Service answered a question from a television writer, did Harding get credit for creating "founding fathers." Given his tattered historical reputation, "founding fathers" may be his most enduring legacy.

"Founding fathers" was tailor-made to evoke an image that artists revisited for more than two centuries. Painters and engravers— John Trumbull and Amos Doolittle in the early Republic; Junius Brutus Stearns in the mid-nineteenth century; Howard Chandler Christy, Henry Hy Hintermeister, and Barry Faulkner in the early twentieth century; Louis Glantzman in the Constitution's bicentennial—depicted the nation's founding moments in standard form: a group of somber politicians in a legislative chamber, focused on a document.

Some of these pictures are patriotic icons, displayed in temples of the nation's civic religion. For example, Trumbull's "The Declaration of Independence" and Christy's "The Signing of the Constitution" hang in the US Capitol; and Barry Faulkner's murals "The Declaration of Independence" and "The Constitution of the United States" loom above visitors to the National Archives, which houses the original Declaration, Constitution, and Bill of Rights. The effect is the same—a staid group of white men, frozen in time.

This conjunction of words and images raises the question of what Harding's phrase means. Most scholars identify as "founding fathers" those who helped to found the United States as a nation and a political experiment. This group has two subsets. First are the Signers, delegates to the Second Continental Congress, who in July 1776 declared American independence and signed the Declaration of Independence. Second are the Framers, the delegates to the Federal Convention who in 1787 framed the Constitution of the United States. At least, the roster includes Benjamin Franklin, George Washington, John Adams, Thomas Jefferson, John Jay, James Madison, and Alexander Hamilton. These men, who played central roles in the American Founding, appear regularly in these pages.

"Founding fathers" is a protean phrase. It can include participants on both sides of the controversy over ratifying the Constitution, as well as those who served in the militia or the Continental Army or Navy during the American Revolution, who elected delegates to the state conventions that ratified the Constitution, and who helped to launch the new government. Writers highlighting women's roles in the nation's history label as "founding mothers" such women as Abigail Adams, Mercy Otis Warren, and Deborah Sampson. Biographers label their subject as a "forgotten founder," a "forgotten founding father," or, in the case of Aaron Burr, a "fallen founder." The phrase often excludes those who were not white, whether African American or Native American.

The founding fathers were a political elite, though a more porous and open elite than those holding sway in Europe. Though seeking to direct the course of events, the founding fathers had to interact with the people, responding to changes coming from below and to shifts in popular opinion. Important studies of the founding fathers have doubted their disinterestedness, highlighting clashes of ideals and concerns between different levels of American society. For these reasons, reconsidering the founding fathers illuminates the evolution of American politics and democracy.

Seeking to order the world with words, the founding fathers created documents of political foundation: constitutions, bills of rights, treaties, and laws. Thus, John Adams rightly called his time "the age of revolutions and constitutions." Ordering the world with words is a theme pervading their writings—and this book. We continue struggling to order the world with words, quarreling over how to interpret their words, seeking to revise or add to the words they left us. Reconsidering the founding fathers helps us to grasp the possibilities and limits of that kind of political thought and action.

This book also examines the founding fathers' legacies and how later generations wrestled with preserving those legacies versus reforming or transforming them to meet changing values and circumstances. We argue about such ideas as liberty, equality, national identity, separation of church and state, and constitutional government in terms devised by the founding fathers. We invoke them as oracles or reject them as irrelevant.

The founding fathers fascinate Americans in all walks of life. Americans celebrate them for erecting for posterity an enduring Constitution and an enduring standard of statesmanship. And yet Americans argue bitterly over why they failed to confront their era's moral issues, such as slavery and its implications for issues of race and equality.

Recent crises have increased reverence for the founding fathers; this is nothing new. In 1941, on the brink of World War II, the novelist and critic John Dos Passos wrote: "In times of change and danger, when there is a quicksand of fear under men's reasoning, a sense of continuity with generations gone before can stretch like a lifeline across the scary present and get us past the idiot delusion of the exceptional." Dos Passos's words apply well to modern times.

The appeal of a mythologized cadre of founding fathers extends beyond the nation's borders. For decades, people around the world have replaced corrupt, oppressive governments with constitutional democracies, seeking guidance from the American founding. This is the latest chapter of a story reaching back to the era of the founding fathers—beginning with French politicians framing the French Declaration of the Rights of Man with guidance from American exemplars (and with discreet assistance from the American minister to France, Thomas Jefferson). The trend continued—in the early nineteenth century, when Latin American republics overthrew Spanish rule; following the Second World War, when European nations shed their colonial empires and African and Asian nations experimented with constitutional self-government; and since 1989, when Eastern European nations rejected dictatorship for constitutional democracy.

Though most nations are parliamentary democracies, a form of government different from that outlined in the US Constitution, they still embrace the idea of a democratic government with a written constitution and bill of rights. The model of "political building" they follow is American, even if they devise their own constitutional architecture. The experiment launched by the founding fathers retains significance at home and abroad.

# Chapter 2
# Contexts: The history that made the founding fathers

The founding fathers lived within and were shaped by three interlocking contexts—the Atlantic world's periphery; the British Empire and its constitutional values; and the intellectual world of the transatlantic Enlightenment.

One episode dramatizes the effects of these contexts. On February 12 and 13, 1766, Benjamin Franklin, standing in the well of the British House of Commons, answered questions from members of Parliament about the effects of the Stamp Act on British North America, hoping that his answers would help persuade Parliament to repeal the Stamp Act.

The man identifying himself as "Franklin, of Philadelphia" was not the genial philosopher of legend. Just sixty, he was the most admired American in the world. Born in Boston, tenth son of a candlemaker, he had worked hard to establish himself. He had lived in London for seven years, showing no desire to return to Philadelphia. A lobbyist for Georgia, Massachusetts, New Jersey, and the Pennsylvania Assembly, he also had risen through the British colonial administration, having become in 1753 joint deputy postmaster-general for North America.

Standing before Parliament, Franklin embodied the three contexts shaping the founding fathers. By his own conduct and example, he tried to transcend the separation of periphery and center overshadowing relations between the American colonies and Britain. He defended the colonists' conception of themselves as freeborn English subjects, even as that conception was provoking crisis within the empire. And he drew much of his authority from his stature as a representative of the Enlightenment, embodying the Enlightenment's hallmark—the pursuit of useful knowledge.

In four hours of testimony over two days, Franklin tried to explain America to Britain. He described the colonists as among the most ardent and loyal subjects of George III. Asked about the American view of Britain before the Stamp Act, he replied:

> The best in the world. They submitted willingly to the government of the Crown, and paid, in all their courts, obedience to acts of Parliament. Numerous as the people are in the several old provinces, they cost you nothing in forts, citadels, garrisons, or armies, to keep them in subjection. They were governed by this country at the expense only of a little pen, ink, and paper. They were led by a thread.

He added that those views since the Stamp Act were "very much altered," and that American respect for Parliament had been "greatly lessened." In one last exchange, he evoked the colonists' determination to resist what they saw as unjust taxation:

Q: What used to be the pride of the Americans?
A: To indulge in the fashions and manufactures of Great Britain.
Q: What is now their pride?
A: To wear their old clothes over again till they can make new ones.

Many observers credited Franklin with swaying Parliament to repeal the Stamp Act.

As Franklin testified before Parliament, other Americans were making their way in the world. George Washington, thirty-three, was a wealthy Virginia planter, remembering his exploits as a colonial militia officer during the French and Indian War and resenting the disdain with which British officers treated him. John Adams, thirty, was a rising member of the Massachusetts bar, married less than two years and pondering how he might advance his career. Thomas Jefferson, twenty-two, was in his last year of study for the Virginia bar, shy and quiet, the protégé of one of the two finest lawyers in the colony. John Jay, twenty, and known for his level-headed dignity, was studying for the bar in New York City, having graduated from King's College. James Madison, fourteen, was excelling in his studies at his father's plantation in Virginia and looking forward to attending college. And Alexander Hamilton, eleven, was a clerk in a shipping firm in Christiansted, on St. Croix in the West Indies, dreaming of achieving fame and glory. Franklin was arguing for all of them, as well as the rest of British North America.

In 1766, Franklin would have deemed the idea of independence incomprehensible. He never expected that the controversy over British taxation of the colonies would tear the British Empire apart, create a new American nation, and transform Franklin from an urbane British imperialist into an American founding father.

## Living on the periphery of the Western world

The America of 1787 was little changed from the America of 1766—except for its constitutional transformation from a collection of colonies to a confederation of states. In May 1787, as Franklin prepared to attend the Federal Convention, the United States occupied almost the same place on the fringe of Atlantic civilization that it had when he had tried to explain the colonies and the mother country to each other.

In 1787, the United States of America had been an independent nation for just over a decade and a nation at peace for less than five years—yet the United States embodied 170 years of Anglo-American political experience. Europeans may have found America rustic and provincial—but Americans had mastered the art of politics, had evolved a thriving and complex society, and were working to forge a national identity.

The most astonishing aspect of the United States was its size. From north to south the new nation spanned 1,200 miles, and from the Atlantic coast to the Mississippi River 600 miles. Most of the American states were as large as a medium-sized European nation; England could have fit within New York State. The United States was blessed with natural resources and room for growth. Even if the American population doubled every twenty years, as Benjamin Franklin predicted in 1751, there was room enough in the new republic for "the thousandth and thousandth generation," as Thomas Jefferson confidently asserted in 1801.

2.  Johann David Schoepf's 1787 map of the Confederation shows the new nation's size, a major challenge facing the founding fathers.

Though the United States was the largest nation in the Western world except Russia, its population was sparse—fewer than four million inhabitants. To the west lay the territory ceded by Great Britain after the Revolution, the domain of Native American nations. The British maintained a military presence there despite the Treaty of Paris of 1783, which required them to evacuate the region; they claimed the right to keep their forts until the Americans met their treaty obligations to repay debts owed to British creditors.

Another factor shaping the United States was its remoteness from Europe. The Atlantic Ocean, a highway of commerce, linked the New World to the Old World, but it also was a barrier, fraught with peril for those who dared to cross it. A ship could take as long as two months to sail between Europe and America. Beyond the separation imposed by geography loomed the difference between the center and the periphery. For those who lived in an imperial European capital, Americans seemed quaint and backward. That sense of difference often took the form of European condescension to Americans, which Americans grew to resent.

Geography shaped a diverse population, from different states and regions, who were all too aware of their diversity and unsure what it portended for creating a nation. From the Albany Congress of 1754 through the Federal Convention of 1787, delegates from different colonies or states observed one another narrowly, penning detailed descriptions of their cultural, religious, and political differences and wondering what weight to give such differences. New England divines, merchants, and lawyers struggled to find common ground with southern planters, and vice versa; and New Englanders and southerners found perplexing the fast-talking commercial entrepreneurs of New York, New Jersey, and Pennsylvania.

Americans were mostly a nation of farmers, although some predicted a glorious future for the United States as a manufacturing and commercial nation. Even those practicing the professions—lawyers, doctors, and the clergy—never fully abandoned farming. Agriculture was central to the American economy. Seven of ten Americans earned their livelihood by working on small farms; three worked on farms owned by others, and four owned the land they tilled. Most farms had 96 to 160 acres, but few acres were in active cultivation; the rest were used for pasture or timber or were left fallow. These farms required the labor of a farmer and his wife, their children, and hired hands—or, in the South, slaves.

Most Americans lived closely tied to the agricultural economy's cycles of plantings and harvests. Farming families rarely saw anyone outside their own household on a daily basis. Sometimes they traveled to the nearest town to buy provisions, sell crops, and learn the news; they might also attend religious services. Their existence was hard, with few amenities, but their standard of living was high—in many ways the highest in the Western world.

Most Americans were not active in politics, contenting themselves with voting if they met state constitutional and legal qualifications. Every state had property tests for voting and higher property qualifications for officeholding. These tests grew out of a basic assumption about politics: one must have a stake in society to be able to vote; only independent voters, who could prove their invulnerability to coercion from employers or landlords by satisfying the property test, should vote. How many Americans met property tests for voting is disputable, though those tests were relatively easy to satisfy.

Few Americans aspired to hold office. Governing American societies were assumptions distilled by the term *deference*. Americans were of two kinds: gentlemen, who had independent incomes not derived from earning a living and thus were suited to hold office, and everyone else, lumped together as "the common sort." The common sort rarely challenged the assumption that politics was an elite matter, but ideas released by the Revolution buffeted deferential society, eroding the distinction between gentlemen and the common sort.

Those distinctions were not rigid, unlike the class barriers found in Europe. A runaway apprentice could relocate from Boston to Philadelphia, becoming wealthy, respected, and powerful. This was Franklin's achievement, evoking the possibilities of America. Similarly, a brilliant, illegitimate child—Alexander Hamilton—could find backing to leave the Caribbean to be educated at King's College (now Columbia University), becoming a war hero, a distinguished attorney, and a leading advocate of a stronger national government.

Religion divided American society, with a staggering diversity of religious beliefs sheltering under the umbrella of Protestant Christianity. Accompanying this diversity were various forms of church-state relations. Some states used taxes to raise funds to support a few sects or denominations; religious tests disqualified members of dissenting sects from holding office. In other states, no sect or denomination received preferred status or taxpayer funds, though nonbelievers deferred to believers. And in Virginia and Rhode Island, absolute religious liberty existed.

Other divisions pervaded American society. Women were the largest group excluded from politics. Statutes or the common law barred single and married women from voting. Under the common-law doctrine of coverture, a married couple constituted one unit for political and economic purposes; only the husband represented the married couple in politics. Even a wife running her own business could not sue or be sued without including her husband as co-plaintiff or co-defendant. Only in New Jersey, from 1776 to 1806, could single women vote.

During and after the Revolution, women took part in politics indirectly—boycotting British goods, preparing supplies for American soldiers, and acting as intelligence gatherers. Mercy Otis Warren wrote pamphlets, including an influential essay opposing the Constitution's ratification, and became one of the Revolution's first historians. Though we do not know other women who took part in the pamphlet wars of the Revolution and early Republic, Warren probably was not unique. Politicians' wives were their principal advisors and sources of information from home. And women were expected to teach their children republican virtue so that their sons would become good citizens and their daughters would continue the tradition of "republican motherhood." Some women, such as Abigail Adams, protested privately that the Revolution ought to "remember the ladies," but their calls went unheeded.

Race, the most visible dividing line, was entangled with the institution of slavery. In 1787, every state but Massachusetts had slavery. Although such northern states as New York had significant numbers of free people of color, ideas about race, slavery, and the link between the two rested on the assumption that whites were superior to blacks. Some slave owners freed slaves, and such religious groups as the Quakers denounced slavery, but there was no organized movement for emancipation or abolition. Such groups as the New York Manumission Society, with John Jay and Alexander Hamilton among its founders, and the Pennsylvania Anti-Slavery Society, founded by Franklin, encouraged action by individual slave owners rather than urging governmental action against slavery as an institution.

In 1775, the African American poet and slave Phillis Wheatley penned verses honoring George Washington, and received his thanks—but she also faced an inquiry by leading figures of Boston to determine whether she wrote her own poetry. In one of the most important American books published before 1800, *Notes on the State of Virginia*, Thomas Jefferson made a "scientific" case for the racial inferiority of those of African descent—an argument stirring little controversy. Though in some states, free African Americans satisfied property qualifications entitling them to vote, they were exceptions. For most Americans, a black skin meant slavery—and racial inferiority, even for free blacks. Most supporters of the Revolution avoided issues of race and slavery, though Washington recognized the incongruousness of the juxtaposition of Americans' objections British attempts to reduce them to a state of slavery with "the blacks we rule over with such arbitrary sway." Opponents of the American Revolution, such as the English literary critic Dr. Samuel Johnson, asked the biting question: "How is it that we hear the loudest yelps for liberty among the drivers of negroes?"

Native American nations also raised troubling questions about the nation's racial makeup. Whoever won the Revolution, Native American nations lost. Those allied with the British were deprived of land, exiled from their ancestral homes, and targeted for reprisal by vengeful Americans. White Americans and state governments violated treaties negotiated between the United States and individual Native American nations; one reason for calling the Federal Convention was to create a general government that could prevent such treaty violations.

Those who felt most passionately about being excluded from public life are least visible to modern eyes: those too poor to have a voice in politics, and those who wrestled with debt. Debtors often demanded that governments ease laws regulating debt. Those who were too poor to vote increasingly criticized the laws barring them from the polls. The Revolution launched "a cautiously transforming egalitarianism" that slowly began to open up American public life to those previously excluded.

The story of the founding fathers unfolded on this crowded stage. They were born into a remarkable variety of families, occupations, religious loyalties, and geographic settings. Some came from the landed gentry and the principal religious denomination, sons of leading families destined to join the ruling elite. Others, born among the middling or common sorts, chose the law or medicine as a professional path to distinction. Still others were born in one part of America but chose to seek their fame and fortune elsewhere. Joining this mix were immigrants from other parts of the British Empire.

The founding fathers knew that they lived on the edge of the Atlantic world. They fretted that Europeans would not respect them as they deserved or would exploit America for European advantage. Their conflicted relationship with the Old World was a key factor shaping their efforts to build a nation. Though aware that they were children of Europe, the founding fathers sought to establish their independence from what Jefferson called "the parent stem."

## Freeborn English subjects

Franklin tried to make one crucial point to Parliament: the bond uniting Americans and Britons was that they were freeborn English subjects. Franklin also sought to explain Americans' deep insecurity about how they were seen within the empire. Franklin was undertaking a perhaps impossible project: to bolster Americans' loyalty to Britain while reminding Britain why being British meant so much to George III's American subjects.

The idea of "the freeborn Englishman" was central to British identity. England's history of civil wars and regicide, culminating in the Glorious Revolution of 1688, resulted in a stable constitutional and political order extolling liberty. England had emerged from the crucible of revolution purified, an orderly polity and society, stable and energetic, rational and enterprising, reaping the rewards of empire. The English attributed this success to their unwritten constitution, a form of government developed over centuries while retaining core principles of liberty.

European and American perceptions of Britain focused on admiration for the English constitution and its protection of liberty.

Though Americans treasured their English constitutional heritage, between 1765 and 1776 that heritage came under siege—from the mother country. The dispute over British colonial policy that sent the British Empire spiraling into civil war was wrenching and unexpected, and Americans searched frantically for an explanation of what had gone wrong.

How did the English constitution apply to Britain's authority over the American colonies? The dispute began when, following the last colonial war between Britain and France, Britain sought to require Americans to assume a share of the financial burden generated by war and defense. The British assumed that, as the war had been fought largely to protect Britain's American colonies from France, Americans ought to help pay for that war. In 1765, Parliament enacted measures taxing the colonists. The most notorious, the Stamp Act, imposed a tax on printed goods, from legal documents to playing cards, symbolized by an affixed stamp. British authorities expected no controversy—nor did Americans residing in London, such as Franklin.

To Britain's surprise, Americans objected to and resisted the Stamp Act. They argued that the tax violated a key constitutional principle—"no taxation without representation." Taxes were constitutional only if those being taxed could elect the legislators taxing them. Rejecting this argument, the British insisted that Parliament represented all of the king's subjects; this *virtual* representation eliminated the need for actual representation.

This dispute forced both sides to a deeper level of argument. The colonists insisted that they had settled an empty North American continent by choice, thus, their ancestors and they had rights equal to those of subjects in the mother country. By contrast, the British insisted that because Britain had conquered North America, the colonists had only those rights that Britain chose to recognize.

These ideas framed eleven years of controversy. After repealing the Stamp Act in 1766, Parliament enacted the Declaratory Act, asserting that it had the right to bind the colonies "in all cases whatsoever." In response, Americans maintained that Parliament was violating another constitutional principle—its restraint on arbitrary (unchecked) power. In theory, the House of Lords or the Crown could check the House of Commons. Because, the Americans contended, neither the king nor the House of Lords was stopping the House of Commons from enacting unconstitutional measures, Parliament was exercising unchecked, arbitrary power.

In vain, British polemicists insisted that the colonists were wrong about the English constitution—that Parliament was not arbitrary but merely supreme, having earned that role by defending English liberty against the tyrannical Charles I and James II. Because Parliament had shown that it could be trusted to defend English liberty, Americans should trust Parliament to exercise authority over them.

The two sides were arguing past each other, each side basing its arguments on one of two conflicting visions of the English constitution. The American version, rooted in the seventeenth century, taught that the English constitution was a restraint on arbitrary power from any institution, even Parliament. By contrast, Britain upheld an eighteenth-century version of the English constitution, focusing on Parliamentary supremacy.

Each set of British taxes and each American episode of resistance raised the dispute's stakes. Following the Stamp Act, Parliament enacted the Townshend Acts in the late 1760s, supplanting them in turn in 1773 with the Tea Act, a statute responding to the East India Company's fiscal crisis and designed to solve an array of problems. A three-penny tax on tea would generate proceeds bolstering the East India Company, raising revenue, and ending disputes between America and Britain—or so the British thought. The American response was the "destruction of the tea" (later dubbed the Boston Tea Party) in December 1773. "Sons of Liberty," costumed as Mohawk warriors, boarded three British tea ships at anchor in Boston Harbor, broke open their holds, and dumped the tea into the harbor.

Parliament, responding with anger to this act of disobedience, enacted statutes to punish the people of Massachusetts. One rescinded the province's charter imposing martial law on Massachusetts and Boston. A second closed the port of Boston to commerce. A third fined the people of Boston to make them pay for the lost tea. These measures, which Americans dubbed the "Intolerable Acts," goaded Americans into calling a Continental Congress to meet in Philadelphia to debate an American response to Britain's assault on American rights.

The British government worried that Americans wanted to sever ties with the empire and become independent. Most colonists rejected this charge; they were proud of their connection to the freest empire on earth and to George III. This loyalty fueled the bitterness of American resentment of British treatment. They saw the mother country as betraying English subjects' most cherished possession—constitutional liberty.

After April 19, 1775, when British forces fired on Massachusetts militia at Lexington and Concord and then suffered a humiliating defeat at that militia's hands, American politicians began to realize that the argument was beyond resolution. Even then, such radical delegates as John Adams could not prevent the Second Continental Congress from making one last appeal to George III. Refusing to receive their Olive Branch Petition, the king proclaimed the colonies out of his allegiance and protection and authorized measures to quell the rebellion. Once news of his refusal and his proclamation reached America in late 1775, independence became the only remaining option—and Americans declared independence. Valuing the constitutional legacy inherited from Britain, American constitution-makers wove principles of that legacy into their new state constitutions as they assumed the burdens of independence—preserving the best of the British constitutional tradition, and feeling the shock of leaving the empire.

Even after winning independence, Americans could not agree how to view Britain. In 1785, presented at court as the first American minister to Great Britain, John Adams assured George III that Americans and Britons could restore "the old good nature and the old good humor between people who, though separated by an ocean, and under different governments, have the same language, a similar religion, and kindred blood." Some Americans agreed. Others, such as Jefferson, concluded that Britain was too corrupt to be treated with anything but suspicion and hostility. This conflict of perceptions shaped Americans' efforts to maintain their independence.

## The great confluence

In February 1766, Franklin had expected that Parliament would give his testimony great weight—in part because of his international reputation as a scientist. It was as Dr. Franklin that he was best known; in 1759, the University of St. Andrews in Scotland had awarded him an honorary doctorate for showing that electricity was a natural phenomenon explicable through the scientific method. For Franklin, electricity symbolized man's efforts to understand and control the natural world. Seeing beyond the consequences of his work for the advancement of scientific knowledge, he used his international reputation as an American scientist to promote recognition that America was a place suitable for expanding human knowledge of the natural world.

While Franklin was testifying before Parliament, Bostonians were reading and debating a pamphlet, *A Dissertation on the Canon and Feudal Law,* published the previous fall. The pamphlet, the first major political work by John Adams, was not a staid, abstract work of historical or legal scholarship. Rather, the young lawyer's vigorous polemic painted a vivid picture of the domination of medieval England by a corrupt aristocracy and a tyrannical Catholic Church using canon law and feudalism as instruments of oppression. Deftly drawing an analogy between those benighted times and British colonial policy, Adams issued a call to a war of words and arguments: "Let us dare to read, think, speak, and write." Adams embodied the spirit of the wide-ranging reading and synthesis so characteristic of the American Enlightenment. Americans heeded his mandate, extending his practice of blending a rich medley of history and philosophy in the service of political, constitutional, and legal reform for decades afterward.

Historians assert the primacy of one or another body of thought or experience in the American Enlightenment—the lessons of the Greek democracies and the Roman Republic; Anglo-American constitutionalism; American colonial political experience and documents of political foundation; civic republicanism; or philosophical ideas from such thinkers as Charles de Montesquieu, David Hume, or John Locke. It is impossible to make a conclusive case for any single candidate. Rather, Americans were influenced by differing constellations of ideas and assumptions; they had in common the habit of gathering and synthesizing bodies of thought; the method was the same but the syntheses were different.

Sir Isaac Newton was the Enlightenment's greatest hero. The man who discovered natural laws governing everything from the heavens to a falling rock and who defined a model of scientific inquiry guiding the rise of science, Newton fired his contemporaries' imaginations. For his epitaph, Alexander Pope composed a couplet: "Nature and nature's laws lay hid in night:/ God said, Let Newton be! and all was light."

The quest for natural laws exemplified by Newton's work—and the work of scientists building on his achievements—inspired daring hopes. If William Herschel could apply Newton's laws to the motions of the six known planets, deduce the existence of a seventh planet, and find it where he said it would appear; if Reverend Joseph Priestley could add oxygen to the chemical elements and Antoine Lavoisier could explain its role in combustion; if Franklin could make of electricity a comprehensible scientific phenomenon—in short, if the age could identify natural laws binding God Himself and His creation, perhaps other thinkers could identify and apply equally binding natural laws regulating human nature, society, politics, and government. This great goal inspired Americans to blend practical politics with inquiries into history, politics, government, and society. Among the ranks of American thinking politicians were leading thinkers of the American Enlightenment—the founding fathers.

The eighteenth century was the last era when one person could master humanity's accumulated wisdom and experience. Philosophers throughout the Western world accepted the challenge, writing treatises on every subject under the sun. Others published multivolume compilations—such as the French Comte de Buffon's *Natural History*, nearly forty volumes plus twelve volumes of engraved plates; Charles Rollin's popular *Ancient History*; and, towering above the rest, the collaborative *Encyclopédie Méthodique* planned and edited by Denis Diderot. The French coined a new word to describe a theorist engaged in reform: *philosophe*.

This intellectual world gave the American colonists the intellectual tools to meet the political, diplomatic, and constitutional challenges facing them when the ties binding them to the empire dissolved. Having won independence, they applied the Enlightenment's lessons to the political and constitutional problems confronting them. Different founding fathers responded to the Enlightenment in different ways. Some, such as Thomas Paine and to a lesser extent Benjamin Franklin, Thomas Jefferson, and Benjamin Rush, saw it as a welcome chance to uproot oppressive old ways. Rush, for example, urged that Americans reform education by dropping the teaching of Latin and Greek as useless rubbish. Others, such as John Adams and Alexander Hamilton, saw the Enlightenment as an opportunity for a gigantic project of sorting human wisdom—identifying and conserving the best of the past while discarding what had to be revised or replaced.

Although the Enlightenment spanned the Western world, different flavors of the movement took form in different nations. The American version of the Enlightenment focused on institutions of government, movements for constitutional and legal reform, and the study of constitutionalism, government, and politics. American literature between the 1760s and the 1800s

3. Coauthor of *The Federalist* and leading diplomat and jurist, John Jay, as the nation's first chief justice, extolled the amending process as a way to adjust the Constitution.

produced such works of political thought and argument as Thomas Paine's *Common Sense,* John Adams's *Thoughts on Government* and *A Defence of the Constitutions of Government of the United States,* J. Hector St. John de Crêvecoeur's *Letters from an American Farmer,* and Thomas Jefferson's *Notes on the State of Virginia.* The literature spawned on both sides of the ratification controversy in 1787–1788 deserves special mention. Though posterity focuses on Alexander Hamilton's, James Madison's, and John Jay's *The Federalist,* the authoritative edition of commentaries on the Constitution during ratification fills six stout volumes, including John Jay's *Address to the People of the State of New-York,* the anonymous *Letters from the Federal Farmer to the Republican,* and the pseudonymous *Letters of Brutus.* Pride in these achievements led Americans to think of their nation as "the empire of reason."

All three contexts—the intellectual context of the Enlightenment; the political context within which Americans sought to preserve and improve the best of Anglo-American constitutional heritage; and the social, economic, and cultural context formed by Americans as a result of living on the Atlantic world's periphery—helped to shape the founding fathers, their sense of their role in American and world history, and their political and constitutional achievements.

# Chapter 3

# Achievements and challenges: The history the founding fathers made

On November 30, 1787, James Madison published *The Federalist No. 14* in *The New-York Packet*; this essay defended the idea of the "extended republic" as justification for the Constitution, a subject raised in *The Federalist No. 10*. He challenged the Constitution's critics:

> But why is the experiment of an extended republic to be rejected merely because it may comprise what is new? Is it not the glory of the people of America, that whilst they have paid a decent regard to the opinions of former times and other nations, they have not suffered a blind veneration for antiquity, for custom, or for names, to overrule the suggestions of their own good sense, the knowledge of their own situation, and the lessons of their own experience? To this manly spirit, posterity will be indebted for the possession, and the world for the example of the numerous innovations displayed on the American theatre, in favor of private rights and public happiness.

Madison's eloquent picture of the founding fathers' relationship with the past defines a valuable perspective for reconsidering them.

The founding fathers engaged in a creative argument between past and present about the future. For seven decades, they played pivotal roles in creating an American nation and its constitutional system. They had no guarantees that their efforts would succeed, and they disagreed about every step taken to achieve independence, nationhood, and constitutional government. Exacerbating these divisions was their belief that not only would their labors determine their own fates and the fates of future generations of Americans; they also hoped to answer affirmatively the question whether, in Alexander Hamilton's words, human beings were "capable or not, of establishing good government by reflection and choice, or whether they were forever destined to depend, for their political constitutions, on accident and force." A wrong choice might become "the general misfortune of mankind."

Two themes undergird the founding fathers' struggles. The first is their sense of *firstness*. When independence became feasible and necessary, they faced the task of defining what it would mean, what kind of independent government they would have, what kind of politics they would practice under that government, and what kinds of laws they would make. The second is their sense of *connectedness* to history and to posterity—to generations gone before and generations yet to come. They linked their sense of being situated in historical time with their belief that theirs was a pivotal era in history. Their sense of firstness did not divorce them from the past nor from the future but rather intensified their connections with past and future.

## Independence

Though they led the first successful colonial revolution against a mother country, many founding fathers reacted with anger against Britain, which had lost its soul and rejected them, forcing them into a dangerous enterprise that might plunge them and America into disaster. Even as their goal shifted from resistance to revolution, Americans knew that the odds were stacked against them—though some put a brave face on the matter. In *Common Sense*, Thomas Paine argued that independence was desirable, well deserved, and feasible; his arguments for independence were

**4. Because war as well as words ordered the political world during the Revolution, the American victory at the Battle of Yorktown was pivotal in creating the United States.**

reasons for his pamphlet's popularity. In later writings, he continued to invoke independence to bolster Americans' commitment to the Revolution.

American commanders paid close attention to the ideological and political goals the war was supposed to achieve, seeking to fix those goals in the minds of the forces they commanded. The war was a learning experience for George Washington and for those he led; he and his soldiers had to overcome parochial loyalties, customs, and habits, and to think of themselves as Americans in a common cause. That Washington, his officers, and his men learned and acted on these lessons was crucial to the Continental Army's victory.

For Washington, the Revolution brought heavy burdens. Not only was he the Continental Army's commander in chief, but he also became the ultimate American symbol, embodying the Revolution in a way that no other founding father could match. The weight of his responsibility proved almost unendurable, yet he struggled to carry it while rejecting the delusion of indispensability that had afflicted such earlier revolutionary leaders as Oliver Cromwell.

In particular, Washington defended the principle that civil authority is rightly superior to military power. In 1783, he thwarted a plan by unpaid, resentful officers to challenge the Confederation Congress's authority; seeing this Newburgh Conspiracy as a dire threat to the American cause, he quelled it by sheer force of personality. In December 1783, after the war's end, he tendered his resignation to the Confederation Congress, emulating the Roman Republic's Lucius Quinctius Cincinnatus, who left his plow to lead Rome's armies and returned to his farm once the crisis had ended.

Washington's resignation became critical to his reputation; his countrymen saw his willingness to yield power as a reason to trust him with power. Reluctantly agreeing in 1787 to attend the Federal Convention, and then backing ratification of the proposed Constitution, Washington discovered that his countrymen wanted to make him their first president; Madison and Hamilton argued that his duty to the Union required him to accept the post. Elected unanimously, he found the presidency a terrible ordeal. In 1792, Jefferson and Hamilton, who by this point agreed on little else, persuaded him to accept a second term. In September 1796, he announced that he would retire from the presidency, creating a two-term tradition that shaped the office for generations. Washington's politics of renunciation helped to define American independence; he confirmed the American commitment to constitutional government in general and the principles of rotation in office and civilian supremacy over military power.

Independence meant more than military victory or legal separation from Britain. What kind of independent entity would the United States be? What kind of government would it have?

These questions focused the founding fathers' attention on devising forms of government for the states, the form of government uniting those states, and the principles governing the new nation's independent course.

Rumors circulated that American leaders wanted to name a monarch, but there was no truth in them. Nonetheless, Americans worried: would the American Revolution merely swap one king for another? If so, why seek independence? Though the threat of an American monarchy hovered on the edge of debate, other issues, far more real, linked discussions of constitution-making to the central issue: would a constitutional government help to maintain American independence?

Defining what independence meant was at the heart of the Declaration of Independence. That document emerged from the resolutions offered on June 7, 1776, by Richard Henry Lee of Virginia. Defining Congress's agenda, the resolutions distilled the formula for independence. The central resolution declared "that these united colonies are, and of right ought to be, free and independent States, that they are absolved from all allegiance to the British Crown, and that all political connection between them and the State of Great Britain is, and ought to be, totally dissolved." Congress debated and adopted it and two other resolutions—one authorizing Congress to name diplomats to win recognition of American independence and treaties of alliance from European nations, and the other authorizing "articles of confederation and perpetual union" to preserve the thirteen states as an American Union.

Congress named three committees—to draft articles of confederation, to plan diplomatic initiatives, and to frame a declaration of independence. The third committee's Declaration, which Congress approved two days after adopting Lee's resolutions, became fused in American memory with the decision to declare independence.

The Declaration was drafted by Thomas Jefferson, with assistance from John Adams and Benjamin Franklin; Congress edited his draft, improving its cogency. The Declaration presented a three-part argument. The first stated principles justifying independence, offering those principles as the basis for an independent America. The second focused on George III, accusing him of violating his kingly responsibilities to his American subjects; in 1776, this indictment was the Declaration's most controversial component. The third declared independence as the justified American response to facts proved in the indictment.

The Declaration was Janus-faced. Like the Roman god of past and future, it looked backward, stating the Americans' last arguments in the dispute with Britain, and it looked forward, defining the principles for which Americans declared independence and by which they would govern themselves. It addressed the American people, "a candid world," and posterity.

Independence also guided American diplomats. Franklin, Adams, and Jay were committed to enlisting European support for the United States, without compromising independence by tying the nation too closely to its allies. The diplomats battled among themselves, sometimes appealing over one another's heads to Congress. Adams charged that Franklin was lazy and that he was too subservient to and bedazzled by France. In response, Franklin described Adams as not just undiplomatic but bullheaded, quarrelsome, parochial, and suspicious—that he was endangering independence by offending France, the nation's greatest ally. Though their disputes threatened to overwhelm their efforts, Franklin and Adams helped to advance American interests in Europe and to aid the war effort. Franklin created the 1778 alliance with France following the American victory in the Battle of Saratoga in 1777; Adams negotiated a treaty with the Netherlands and arranged loans from Dutch bankers to Congress to help finance the American cause.

Joining Adams and Franklin in Paris, John Jay tipped the scales. Cooler than Adams, warier of the French than Franklin, he helped to set in motion the negotiations with Britain and to define their tone. (The diplomats saddled Franklin with the delicate task of explaining to the French why the Americans had made peace with Britain without consulting them.) The Treaty of Paris of 1783 realized the American vision of independence. Accepting American independence, the British ceded to the United States all territory between the Allegheny Mountains and the Mississippi River, a cession building westward expansion into the American future.

Even after the Treaty of Paris, independence remained only a legal and diplomatic fact. The new nation still suffered from economic and political vulnerabilities threatening to undermine independence. In the 1780s, supporters and opponents of strengthening American government divided over how to preserve independence; this division became acute in the struggle over ratifying the Constitution. Supporters of the Constitution insisted that it had to be adopted because a government too weak to protect American interests would sacrifice independence. By contrast, their adversaries argued that Americans had revolted against a strong, distant government—like that sketched in the Constitution; this new government would devour liberty and create a tyranny that would destroy independence.

Independence remained a touchstone for national politics after the Constitution's adoption. Americans used concepts of independence and the Revolution interchangeably, regarding a threat to one as a threat to the other. Federalists and Republicans claimed to be the Revolution's guardians, denouncing their foes as endangering independence. In 1793, Federalists and Republicans divided over whether the United States should stay neutral in the wars convulsing Europe or take sides with Revolutionary France against the league of conservative monarchies led by Britain. Republicans invoked the French-American alliance's essential role in winning independence. Federalists answered that Louis XVI's execution in 1792 abrogated that alliance, and that the United States had to maintain neutrality to preserve its independence.

Arguments invoking independence persisted into the nineteenth century, especially during the War of 1812. Republicans saw that struggle as a second war for independence against Britain; Federalists denounced the conflict as endangering independence. The controversy became so bitter that some Federalists discussed taking their states out of the Union and forming a separate confederation or seeking to return to the British Empire. Only the Treaty of Ghent of 1815, followed by General Andrew Jackson's victory in the Battle of New Orleans, derailed these enterprises of disunion threatening independence.

From the 1760s to the 1820s, independence evolved from goal (in the 1770s and early 1780s), to an achievement requiring defense (from the late 1780s to the early 1800s), to an assumed fact (after the War of 1812). Jefferson's last public letter, written ten days before his death (on the Declaration's fiftieth anniversary), makes that evolution clear. Calling the Declaration "an instrument pregnant with our own, and the fate of the world," and noting that in 1776 Congress faced "the bold and doubtful election we were to make, for our country, between submission, or the sword," Jefferson expressed his happiness that posterity continued "to approve the choice we made." He then set the Declaration in the context of world history:

> May it be to the world what I believe it will be, (to some parts sooner, to others later, but finally to all), the Signal of arousing men to burst the chains, under which monkish ignorance and superstition had persuaded them to bind themselves, and to assume the blessings & security of self government. That form which we have substituted restores the free right to the unbounded exercise of reason and freedom of opinion. All eyes are opened, or opening to the rights of man. The general spread of the light of science has already laid open to every view the palpable truth, that the mass of mankind has not

been born, with saddles on their backs, nor a favored few booted and spurred, ready to ride them legitimately, by the grace of god. These are grounds of hope for others. For ourselves, let the annual return of this day for ever refresh our recollections of these rights, and an undiminished devotion to them.

## Constitution-making

Americans gave enduring meaning to independence by creating state and national constitutions. The founding fathers sought to re-establish lawful government, which had collapsed in 1775–1776 with the breakdown of British rule; they also sought to safeguard independence, to give it institutional form, and to define what it would mean.

A revolution succeeds only if it replaces an unjust existing order with a new, more just order. On June 28, 1787, Franklin used the phrase "political building" in a speech to the Federal Convention to evoke revolution's constructive component. The era of political building resulted in an array of written constitutions, for the states and for the United States. This achievement had two linked parts: the constitutions and the means of framing and adopting them.

Constitution-making was an American problem even before independence. In mid-1775, royal colonial officials fled their posts, creating a void of legitimate government. To fill this void, the people of each colony accepted leadership by provincial congresses and conventions—but these arrangements were temporary. Seeking a way to restore lawful government, Americans recalled their colonial charters granted by the mother country. These charters had organized colonial politics; legislatures used them to evaluate actions by royal governors and Crown officials. In an untried political world, Americans realized, framing and adopting a written constitution might replace the charters that had organized their political lives as legitimate.

What should a state constitution provide? How should it be framed and adopted? To answer these questions, American politicians turned to John Adams of Massachusetts, renowned for his constitutional learning. Deluged with appeals for advice, he wrote many letters sketching a design for a constitution. Finally, in April 1776, he reworked one letter as a pamphlet, *Thoughts on Government*, which was his most influential work.

Writing to James Warren that his "Design [in writing *Thoughts on Government*] is to mark out a Path, and putt Men upon thinking," Adams embraced the chance to distill his study of constitutional government. Besides wanting to guide American efforts at constitution-making, Adams hoped to counter a prescription for new state governments set forth by Thomas Paine's *Common Sense*. Adams valued Paine's arguments for independence and his plain-spoken eloquence—but Paine's rejection of checks and balances and separation of powers horrified him.

Paine saw the idea of a two-house legislature balanced by a powerful executive as an unnecessary throwback, echoing the British model of King, Lords, and Commons. He argued that if the people were to have ultimate political power, there was no need to protect themselves from themselves. To Paine, such doctrines were mystifications putting government beyond popular understanding, reserving it for the educated and wealthy, who would keep themselves in power at the people's expense.

In turn, Paine's ideas offended Adams. History, Adams insisted, taught that the people could be as oppressive as a king or an aristocracy; only a checked and balanced government could prevent such oppression. Adams proposed precisely the model of a state constitution that Paine spurned, one including a bicameral legislature, a powerful governor, and checks and balances.

During the Revolution, Americans adopted an array of state constitutions. The models offered by Paine and Adams formed the poles of a spectrum of experiments in government. In Connecticut and Rhode Island, the legislatures revised their colonial charters, deleting all references to England and the king; the revised charters served as constitutions into the nineteenth century. In the other eleven states, new constitutions supplanted colonial charters.

These experiments in government formed two great waves of Revolutionary state constitution-making. First-wave constitution-makers favored a powerful legislature with feeble executive and judicial institutions; they cared little about how to frame and adopt a constitution. A provincial congress or convention would assert the power to frame a constitution, draft it, and declare it in effect (or call for elections, announcing that those elected would serve under the new constitution).

The written bill of rights was the enduring, influential product of this first wave. Virginia's 1776 constitution began with a declaration of rights penned by George Mason; James Madison assisted on the religious liberty provision. This much-imitated declaration, codifying right principles instead of judicially enforceable rights, was to guide voters in evaluating their elected officials.

Despite the popularity of written bills of rights, a reaction set in against this first wave of Revolutionary constitutionalism. In New York (1777), and in Massachusetts (1779–1780), constitution-makers devised a competing model of constitutional government. New York's constitution created a governor, elected by the people for three years, with powers (shared with a Council of Revision and a Council of Appointment) to veto legislation and appoint executive officials. The framers of the New York constitution scattered rights-declaring provisions through the document.

Massachusetts extended New York's achievements by devising a new way to frame and adopt a constitution. In 1778, the state legislature declared that the next election would empower it to draft a constitution. The legislature sent that draft constitution to the state's town meetings for the voters' approval—the first time that a constitution was submitted to the people. The town meetings rejected the constitution by nearly four to one—denouncing its malapportionment of the legislature; its lack of a bill of rights; and its failure to establish separation of powers. Chastened, the legislature called elections for a new convention, which would have the sole task of drafting a constitution to be submitted to the town meetings. Massachusetts thus invented the constitutional convention.

The convention's delegates chose a drafting committee—James Bowdoin, Samuel Adams, and John Adams—which assigned the task of drafting to John Adams, He produced the most eloquent of the state constitutions. It is impossible to determine whether the convention edited his draft, for all we have is the final version. Over several months, the towns debated the draft constitution clause by clause and prepared reports indicating what parts they approved, what they rejected, and why. In October 1780, after sifting these reports, the convention declared every provision of the constitution adopted by the needed two-thirds majority. On October 25, 1780, the new constitution of Massachusetts went into effect.

These constitution-making experiments helped to define what kind of independence Americans would have. Drawing on the teachings of Montesquieu's *The Spirit of the Laws* and on decades of political experience, Americans recognized a direct relationship between the nature of society and the kind of government it should have, the values government would foster, and the purposes government would seek to achieve.

By contrast with the sophistication of the states' experiments in government, the creation of the Articles of Confederation, the first form of government for the United States, was crude and jury-rigged. Framed in 1777 and adopted in 1781 by all thirteen states, it was not even in effect before critics suggested revising or replacing it.

The Articles created a fragile government with one institution, the Confederation Congress (a reformulated Continental Congress). Each state had one vote in Congress, which had little power. The Confederation Congress deserves credit for many successes. It fielded an army that won the War for Independence (with French aid), and a team of diplomats who made alliances, secured funding for the Union, and negotiated a successful peace treaty. Further, it devised a system for administering the western lands won from Britain under the 1783 peace treaty. These western lands would be organized into territories that would join the Union as states equal in status to the original thirteen. Nonetheless, the problems facing the Confederation raised doubts whether Americans could preserve the Revolution's principles and its greatest achievements—independence, liberty, and Union.

American politicians who struggled to find the best way to answer that question saw that the United States needed a stronger government than the one outlined by the Articles, but they resisted consolidating the states under one national government. Nobody thought that a unified nation as large as the United States could keep its liberty. Even the word "nation" terrified all but Alexander Hamilton, a vehement advocate of national power. Americans preferred strengthening the general government. How could they create a general government able to defend American interests against European powers, or one having power to act on individual citizens without endangering their liberties or the states' powers?

These questions faced the delegates to the Federal Convention in Philadelphia in 1787. At first, the delegates had to decide whether they would even be a constitutional convention—a body having the power to create a constitution. Half the states had chosen delegates to the Convention believing that it would only propose amendments to the Articles. Only after they decided that the Articles needed replacement rather than revision did the delegates vote to become a constitutional convention. Even then, they could only propose a constitution. The power to constitute a government rested with the people of the United States.

Wrestling with these challenges, the delegates to the Convention had available the state constitutions—particularly those of New York and Massachusetts—as prototypes to guide their efforts. Further, they never forgot a central lesson about constitutional design—that a constitution grants power as well as limiting it. The challenging task facing them was to empower a new government for the United States while also limiting its powers.

Creating constitutions at state and national levels divided Americans, including the founding fathers. Adams denounced Paine and Franklin for spurning separation of powers and checks and balances; he rejected the Pennsylvania constitution of 1776 for having a one-house legislature with no separate executive or judicial institutions to check it. At the same time, Madison, who viewed skeptically the power of a bill of rights to protect liberty, disagreed with Jefferson, who insisted on the need for a bill of rights. And many leaders of the Revolution could not agree on how much power to give to the general government. These disagreements sparked profound debates about the nature of liberty and power, the design of a constitution, and the way to frame and adopt a constitution.

Since ancient times, most constitutions had been creations of one lawgiver, the most famous being Solon of Athens, Lycurgus of Sparta, and Publius Valerius Publicola of Rome. By contrast, the American experiments in government were products of collective deliberation.

In four months, working under a rule of secrecy, the Convention's delegates struggled to devise a constitution. The delegates fought the conventional wisdom that so large a nation as the United States could not have a republican government, which was suited only for a small territory whose inhabitants knew one another and had a narrow range of interests. They also tried to balance experience and theory in constitution-making. Should they apply the lessons of history, or should they argue with the past? Should they frame the best constitution that human wisdom could contrive or the best constitution that had a chance of being adopted?

The ratification of the US Constitution in 1787–1788 was even more historic than the Federal Convention; for the first time, the people of a country had the chance to decide how to govern themselves. The Constitution's ratification took place at state and national levels, within formal institutions of government and in the realm of public opinion. The process unfolded as specified in Article VII of the Constitution. The Convention sent the Constitution to the Confederation Congress, which debated it for three days. Though Congress neither endorsed nor condemned the Constitution, Congress endorsed its legitimacy by referring it to the states. Every state but Rhode Island authorized elections of state ratifying conventions. These conventions met in public to debate the Constitution, often clause by clause. Ratification by nine states was needed to put the Constitution into effect—a supermajority hard to achieve but easier than the consent of all thirteen state legislatures needed to amend the Articles.

In each state, furious debate raged over the Constitution. Its opponents demanded that it be rewritten or amended, whereas its supporters insisted that it must be accepted as it was. The major issues were the Constitution's lack of a bill of rights, its grants of power to Congress to regulate interstate and foreign commerce, its methods of representing the people, its creation of a one-man chief executive with generous powers and the ability to be reelected without limit, and its creation of a system of federal courts. The Constitution's opponents denounced it as a threat to liberty for lacking a bill of rights. They worried that Congress's powers were too broad and could endanger state interests, that Congress would not truly represent the American people, that the president might become a king, and that the federal courts would swallow up the state courts and restrict ordinary people's access to the courts.

The Constitution's supporters argued at first that a bill of rights was not needed because the federal government had no power to endanger liberty. They defended Congress's grants of powers as the minimum needed to preserve the Union and safeguard American interests, and they praised the system of congressional representation. They maintained that the president would never become a king, because his powers were far less than those of a king, and they insisted that federal courts were needed to defend the Constitution and federal law from encroachments by the states.

Five states adopted the Constitution by early 1788; the sixth convention, Massachusetts, ground to a halt. The deadlock arose because the Constitution's opponents wanted the document revised before they would approve it and its supporters rejected changes. A compromise emerged to break the deadlock: a list of amendments to be recommended to the first Congress under the Constitution. This idea of recommended amendments prevailed in every ratifying convention following Massachusetts (except South Carolina), allowing the Constitution's opponents to save face, and offering the promise that the Constitution would be amended. Most of the recommended amendments concerned a federal bill of rights—answering the strongest argument against the Constitution. Making the plan of recommended amendments possible was the amending process codified in Article V of the Constitution.

On June 25, 1788, the ninth state convention, New Hampshire, ratified the Constitution, which became the new form of government of the United States. Virginia and New York ratified it later in 1788. North Carolina and Rhode Island held out until 1789 and 1790, respectively, demanding a bill of rights and other amendments.

Surrounding formal political institutions in the adoption of the Constitution was a war of words and arguments, spawning publications from learned pamphlets to newspaper essays to wall posters. These publications for and against the Constitution helped to unite the people in a shared argument about the Constitution. Thus, ratification bolstered American national identity; the people of each state knew that their decision on the Constitution would affect fellow citizens in other states. That realization taught the people to see themselves as citizens of a new American nation, strengthening the bonds of Union.

Further, the political process of ratification and the arguments in print over the Constitution expanded the set of Americans who took part in politics beyond the "better sort." Every literate American had at least some role to play. States suspended property qualifications for voting, allowing every adult male to choose delegates to the ratifying conventions. After ratification ended, Americans beyond the governing elite began to be more active in public life.

In June 1789, James Madison, now a representative from Virginia in the First Federal Congress, became the leading advocate of constitutional amendments, helping to direct the last stage of the ratification controversy. He distilled from over two hundred recommended amendments a list of rights-protecting amendments that omitted anything that would endanger the just powers of the general government. After months of debate, Congress sent twelve proposed amendments to the states, ten being what we now call the Bill of Rights. These proposals persuaded North Carolina to ratify the Constitution in November 1789; Rhode Island reluctantly followed in June 1790. Meanwhile, the other states ratified the Bill of Rights; Virginia's ratification added the first ten amendments to the Constitution on December 15, 1791.

Whether led by or arguing with the founding fathers, Americans showed the world how to make and adopt constitutions and what they should contain. By the 1830s, when the last of the founding fathers died, state constitution-making was a familiar process. On the national level, the Constitution of 1787 became a focus of popular reverence, with little pressure to replace it. Instead, Americans worked sometimes to change the Constitution's text by amending it through the document's amending process, which required a consensus on the problem and on how to solve it. Because it was hard to achieve such a consensus, only two amendments joined the Constitution between the adoption of the Bill of Rights in 1791 and the end of the Civil War in 1865. Amendment XI (1795) declared that no state could be sued in federal court, and Amendment XII (1804) required electoral votes to be cast separately for president and vice president.

Two other forms of constitutional change supplement the amending process. The first is judicial interpretation of the Constitution. The second is the informal method known as custom and usage, which fleshes out the skeleton of government authorized by the Constitution. These methods of constitutional change have helped to keep the Constitution adaptable.

## Courts and judicial power

Courts have been central to American constitutional government since the founding, because of their importance to interpreting the Constitution and adjudicating cases arising under it. To the extent that they agreed on anything, most founding fathers thought that federal courts had the power and responsibility to interpret the Constitution and apply it to disputes brought before them. Even such a vigorous later critic of the Supreme Court as Thomas Jefferson argued to James Madison in 1789 that one strong reason to add a bill of rights to the Constitution was the checking power that it would give to the federal judiciary.

Courts—authorized in Article III—thus were integral to the Constitution, though the framers only gave the federal judiciary a relatively narrow grant of judicial power, or jurisdiction, over certain kinds of cases. Except for specifying that "one supreme Court" would head the judiciary, the Convention left designing the federal courts to the first Congress under the Constitution. In part this decision may have reflected the framers' weariness and desire to be finished; but also in part this decision continued state constitution-makers' preference to leave designing state court systems to statutes enacted by state legislatures.

Opponents and even some supporters of the Constitution questioned the need for federal courts. George Mason of Virginia argued that federal courts would endanger the people's access to the law, swallowing up state courts and rendering law "tedious, intricate, and expensive." By contrast, John Rutledge of South Carolina argued in the Convention that state courts could adjudicate disputes arising under federal law or the Constitution, making the creation of federal courts unnecessary.

Insisting on the federal judiciary's necessity and utility, Hamilton devoted six essays to the subject in *The Federalist*. Rejecting charges that federal courts would be dangerous to state courts or unnecessary because of the existence of state courts, Hamilton insisted that federal courts would perform needed and useful functions; they would ensure uniform interpretations of federal law and defend the Constitution against efforts to undermine or violate it.

In particular, Hamilton made the case for what we call the doctrine of judicial review. He justified two kinds of judicial review—federal/federal or coequal judicial review, in which a federal court assesses the constitutionality of acts by other parts of the federal government (in *The Federalist* No. 78), and federal/ state or supervisory judicial review (in *The Federalist* Nos. 80–82), in which a federal court assesses the constitutionality of state governmental acts. Federal/state judicial review has a clear anchor in the constitutional text, the supremacy clause in Article VI of the Constitution, which makes the Constitution the supreme law of the land and binds state judges to obey it. Federal/federal judicial review has a less clear anchor in the same clause—in the phrase identifying "all laws made under [the Constitution's] authority" as the supreme law of the land under the Constitution. To give a federal law that authority, a court assesses whether that law has been made under the Constitution's authority—that is, whether it is constitutional.

After the Constitution went into effect, the First Federal Congress set to work designing the federal judiciary; the Senate—specifically Senators William Paterson of New Jersey and Oliver Ellsworth and William Samuel Johnson of Connecticut—took the lead in crafting the Judiciary Act of 1789. Once it was enacted into law, President Washington then appointed all federal judges authorized by the new statute.

The Judiciary Act of 1789 created a federal judiciary with three levels. At the pyramid's apex was the "one supreme Court" required by the Constitution, with a chief justice and five associate justices. At the pyramid's base were district courts—one for each state, and one for Kentucky (then part of Virginia) and Maine (then part of Massachusetts), each staffed by one US district judge. Comprising the pyramid's middle layer were the federal circuit courts. The statute divided the country into three groups of states, or circuits—Eastern (New England plus New York), Middle (New Jersey to Virginia), and Southern (the Carolinas and Georgia). Two Supreme Court justices would be assigned to each circuit and "ride circuit" (a term borrowed from England) twice a year, holding circuit court in each state with its US district judge. The district courts had narrow jurisdiction over revenue and customs cases; the circuit courts could hear appeals from the district courts and had their own grant of trial jurisdiction; the Supreme Court had a grant of appellate jurisdiction over the circuit courts and "original jurisdiction" over a small set of cases that could begin in the Supreme Court itself. Chief Justice John Jay and Associate Justice James Wilson were the leading members of the Supreme Court.

The federal circuit courts made the first major judicial decisions interpreting the Constitution. One ruling in Connecticut in 1790 struck down a state statute for violating the ban in the Treaty of Paris of 1783 on state laws interfering with British creditors' ability to collect their just debts from state debtors; that statute prevented accrual of interest on such debts for the period of the War for Independence. Another ruling in Rhode Island in 1792 struck down a state statute as violating the Constitution's clause enforcing the obligations of contracts; that statute required creditors to accept inflated Rhode Island paper money as sole payment for debt owed by Rhode Island debtors. In 1795, in *Hylton v. United States*, the Supreme Court upheld a federal tax on carriages as constitutional, implying that it could have found the statute unconstitutional. In 1803, in *Marbury v. Madison*, the Supreme Court, under its fourth chief justice, John Marshall, struck down a federal statute expanding the Supreme Court's original jurisdiction beyond the limits set by the Constitution's Article III; *Marbury* confirmed the Court's power of judicial review of acts of Congress. Other cases, notably *McCulloch v. Maryland* (1819) and *Fletcher v. Peck* (1810), confirmed the Court's power of judicial review over federal acts and over state acts.

This catalogue of cases does not do justice to the complicated history of the federal courts in the early Republic. Controversy swirled around the courts; the first amendment to the Constitution after the Bill of Rights overturned the Court's 1793 decision, *Chisholm v. Georgia* (which had allowed federal courts to hear lawsuits against a state brought by citizens of another state or subjects of foreign countries). By the early nineteenth century, the federal judiciary had established its authority. Over more than two centuries, with recurring bouts of controversy about its

5. The fourth and greatest chief justice of the United States, John Marshall, made the Supreme Court a powerful and respected institution in the constitutional system.

decisions, the judiciary has continued to be a necessary and respected part of the constitutional system conceived by the founding fathers. And yet the argument over judicial review continues—whether it is anti-democratic, whether it is part of the Constitution, whether the founding fathers intended it or would be aghast at what courts have since done with it.

## Federalism

Federalism may be the US Constitution's most creative feature, but it was the product of amassed individual decisions by the Constitution's framers, not a carefully designed system of relations between the federal government and the states. Devising a form of government to hold the thirteen states together was a greater challenge, as we have seen, than writing individual state constitutions.

The two contrasting extremes among the possible models for such a government—allowing each state to go its own way versus fusing them into one consolidated nation—seemed equally unsatisfactory. The thirteen states could not "go it alone," trusting that their common cause and common interests would hold them together. In the first American political cartoon, published in 1754, Benjamin Franklin gave memorable form to the phrase "JOIN OR DIE"—showing a dead snake cut into segments, each labeled to represent a different colony. That symbol reminded Americans what they risked if they chose to let the Union fall apart. Most Americans agreed that the other extreme—welding the states into one republic—was impossible. Classical political thought taught that a republican government (the only type of government that could preserve liberty) would not work for a large territory; a republic that was too big might collapse into anarchy or tyranny. As the largest state, Virginia, was at the outside limit of the size suitable for a republican government, how could all thirteen states have one government?

The option we know—two levels of government, with each state government managing its own concerns, but deferring to a general government on questions of shared interest—seems a natural solution. At the time, this option clashed with another axiom of conventional political wisdom: two sovereign governments cannot operate in the same territory. Designing a republican government for an American Union became the central constitutional problem of the 1780s.

Americans had three precedents for creating an inter-colonial union, all driven by the need to unite against the French and their Native American allies. The New England Confederation of 1643 united Massachusetts Bay, Plymouth, Connecticut, and New

Haven in a defensive alliance. A council of eight commissioners, two from each colony, oversaw a treasury financed by contributions from each colony's legislature, which also provided militia units for common defense. Though it worked well, the Confederation eroded under the pressure of external events, such as the absorption of New Haven by Connecticut and Plymouth by Massachusetts-Bay. It dissolved in 1684.

Between 1686 and 1688, James II imposed one government on the colonies. He said that he wanted to coordinate colonial defense, but he also rejected colonial legislatures' identifications with Parliament and resistance to royal authority. Revoking colonial charters, he promulgated the Dominion of New England, uniting under one authority (a royal governor with an appointed council) the New England colonies, New York, and the two colonies comprising New Jersey. This plan stimulated colonial resentment and resistance. In 1689, learning of the overthrow of James II in the Glorious Revolution, Americans overthrew and arrested the Dominion's royal governor. King William III and Queen Mary annulled the Dominion and restored the colonies' charters.

The third scheme of inter-colonial union, the Albany Plan of Union of 1754, again resulted from efforts to coordinate colonial defense. In 1754, New York's royal governor, Sir William Johnson, convened a congress at Albany. Massachusetts, New Hampshire, Connecticut, Rhode Island, New York, Pennsylvania, and Maryland sent delegates, as did the Iroquois Confederacy. Reworking a plan proposed by Benjamin Franklin, a Pennsylvania delegate, the Albany Congress submitted it to the Crown and to the colonies. It would have created a president general named by the Crown and a council whose members would be chosen by colonial legislatures under a rule of representation based on taxes paid by each colony to the union. Crown and colonies both rejected the Albany Plan. The Crown resented any plan diminishing its sovereignty; colonial legislatures resisted any plan reducing their authority. Disappointed by his plan's failure,

Franklin later wrote that had the Albany Plan been adopted, it might have prevented the Revolution.

In the 1760s and 1770s, American colonists recognized that resistance to British policy would require union. The first inter-colonial resistance effort, the Stamp Act Congress, met in New York City in 1765. Its successor, the First Continental Congress, convened in Philadelphia's Carpenters Hall in 1774. These congresses met at first to counter specific crises—but when the First Continental Congress completed its business, it voted to convene a Second Continental Congress in early 1775 to pursue further remedies if needed. That spring, British forces and Massachusetts militia exchanged fire at Lexington and Concord. These events persuaded at least some American politicians that a more permanent body should oversee American resistance.

Congress tried to keep pace with the worsening crisis between Britain and America. By July 4, 1776, when Congress proclaimed the Declaration of Independence, it had become a de facto American government. Under prodding by John Adams, the Second Continental Congress also directed the colonies to write new state constitutions. Still, the challenge of a new American government posed difficult problems of theory and practice; these difficulties shaped the creation, between 1777 and 1781, of the Articles of Confederation.

The Articles hamstrung the Confederation in dealing with state governments; the Confederation had no power to coerce states to comply with its requisitions of money, nor to force states to obey treaties made by the Confederation. These concerns animated the national reform effort seeking to revise or replace the Confederation.

The difficulties of crafting a government overseeing thirteen states preoccupied the delegates to the Federal Convention in trying to replace the Confederation, as did such problematic questions as that of representation. Large states demanded a two-house legislature based on population, wealth, or taxes paid to the general government. Small states insisted on equality of state representation. The compromise—one house preserving state equality and the other based on proportional representation—required tough-minded bargaining to induce delegates from the large states to accept it. Once the Convention adopted this compromise, small-state delegates backed giving a surprising amount of authority to the general government; large-state delegates resisted attempts to expand the general government's authority.

The construction of the Constitution and of what became federalism dominated the Convention's second half. As the delegates worked, federalism evolved bit by bit until, after the Convention's end, the delegates started to see its shape and workings. The Constitution's defenders hailed federalism as a way to balance relations between the federal government and the states. In *The Federalist* No. 39, Madison argued that the Constitution defined a middle ground between national and federal government, mixing the best elements of both and avoiding the drawbacks of either. In Pennsylvania's ratifying convention, James Wilson praised the Constitution for creating "a federal republic"; this new form of government, he argued, would prevent states from eroding the general government's authority or the general government from crushing the states. In a federal republic, the American people were the sovereigns, with the states and the general government as their servants.

Among the founding fathers, an array of clashing understandings of federalism emerged. Alexander Hamilton defined the nationalist view. Insisting in *The Federalist* No. 85 that "a NATION without a NATIONAL government" was "an AWFUL spectacle," he worked hard for broad construction of the Constitution, arguing that any power of the general government implied from the words of the Constitution and not explicitly banned by any constitutional provision was legitimate. His goal was to win the greatest scope of power for the general government consistent with the Constitution.

By contrast, Thomas Jefferson at first welcomed federalism. On December 20, 1787, after receiving a copy of the Constitution, he wrote to James Madison: "I am captivated by the compromise of the opposite claims of the great & little states, of the latter to equal, and the former to proportional influence." As a diplomat, he favored vindicating the general government's authority and inducing the states to cooperate with the United States in meeting American obligations to foreign creditors. When he pondered the development of the federal system and the federal government's power to command the states, he reconsidered.

From the early 1790s to the end of his life, Jefferson insisted that giving the general government power to coerce the states would betray the Revolution, substituting coercion for consent. He argued for strict construction of the Constitution: any power not explicitly authorized by the Constitution was unconstitutional. In 1798, Jefferson even insisted that a state nullify within its borders an unconstitutional federal law. And yet President Jefferson expanded federal constitutional power by negotiating the Louisiana Purchase in 1803 and enforcing his embargo on trade with France and Britain in 1807–1808.

Other founding fathers espoused views of federalism that fell between Hamilton's and Jefferson's positions. George Washington tilted strongly in Hamilton's favor on the question of national power versus state sovereignty. So, too, did John Jay, until the War of 1812 made him doubt the federal government; he saw the war as unfairly damaging the interests of New York and other northern states. John Adams also tilted in the direction of national power, but he never grasped federalism as a constitutional principle, because in the 1770s and 1780s he had been in Europe on diplomatic missions and thus had had no direct experience of balancing competing claims of federal and state authority.

By contrast, James Madison became the leading American expert on federalism, having amassed extensive experience dealing with issues of federal versus state authority. Madison shifted his intellectual weight to oppose what he deemed to be any threat to the constitutional system, whether the injustice and mutability of state laws in the 1780s or the federal government's growing power in the 1790s. Rejecting charges that he was inconsistent, he insisted that his constitutional values had never changed. For example, he saw no clash between his demands to place limits on state powers in the 1780s and his embrace of schemes of state power to check federal power in 1798. Over time, his understanding of the line between federal and state authority became so nuanced that, in his old age, advocates of national power and state sovereignty alike criticized him. Each side offered black-and-white readings of federalism and inflexible allegiance to federal power or to state sovereignty—positions that Madison could not share.

Issues of federalism roiled national politics; advocates of federal power and state sovereignty struggled to push the constitutional system to an uncompromising position one way or the other. Every constitution includes issues contested on a case-by-case basis; trying to force a clear solution might trigger conflict that could blow the system apart. Such abeyances absorb the strains that might damage the constitutional system beyond repair. The danger lies in trying to force the solution.

The history of the Constitution between its adoption in 1787 and the Civil War's outbreak in 1861 reveals increasing tension over federalism. Though the constitutional abeyance on federal versus state authority allowed compromises averting conflict, sooner or later a controversy would spin out of control. The sectional crises of the 1820s, 1830s, and 1850s tested federalism almost to the breaking point. The crisis of 1861 shattered the Constitution of 1787 and the Union it was designed to preserve. Ironically, the constitutional system's containment of disunion enabled the federal government to amass enough constitutional authority and military and economic power to preserve the Union when secession finally came. The cost of maintaining the Union was a terrible civil war.

## Politics

Americans faced the challenge of making constitutional systems work in ordinary politics. They devised new means of conducting politics and creatively adapting existing means of political advocacy and action. This story's theme is the evolution of a shifting balance between leadership by enlightened statesmen and insistence by the people that they should play an active role in governance. A byproduct of this tension was the development of political parties, which proved essential to the constitutional system's success. Parties, paradoxically, emerged from a world seeing parties as dangerous conspiracies against the general good.

Though experienced politicians within their states, Americans had little or no experience working together across state lines, even within a legislative body. Organizing the Revolution and running the Confederation were learning experiences, and the Federal Convention was even more so—especially for Madison, who had to confront the challenges of functioning as a legislative leader in a diverse, quarrelsome constitutional convention or legislature. By contrast, the most extreme nationalist among the Convention's delegates, Alexander Hamilton, did not learn that lesson, though he helped to teach it to Madison by criticizing Madison's ideas.

Ten days after the Convention's end, Hamilton and Madison, sitting in the Confederation Congress and astonished by the hostility with which some colleagues viewed the proposed Constitution, agreed to work together to get it ratified. They echoed many speakers during the Convention's last day, who confessed their disappointment with the Constitution yet pledged nonetheless to work for its adoption as the proposal that had the best chance of success.

Ratifying the Constitution blended old and new methods of politics. For example, the tool that Madison and Hamilton used to make their most elaborate case for the Constitution was print—an efficient means of practicing politics in the eighteenth century. *The Federalist* began as a newspaper column appearing twice a week in New York's newspapers; it was only one (though the most sophisticated) of hundreds of pamphlets, essays, and other printed arguments for and against the Constitution. Ratifying the Constitution helped to rewrite the rules of American politics. The state ratifying conventions met in public view, assembling as many as two hundred delegates, with galleries for spectators. Printers published their attempts to record those debates. The openness of the ratifying debates set a precedent for legislative bodies to have galleries where citizens and journalists could observe the proceedings—the first stirrings of the public's right to know. The ratifying conventions resembled popular seminars on constitutional government; advocates on both sides tried to direct the discussion but knew that they could not force the delegates into agreement. These conventions presaged the people's willingness to express their views on political measures, to organize to advance those views, and to challenge the new nation's political leadership.

This turbulent political world required the new nation's leaders to practice a kind of politics resembling and diverging from today's politics. Given that Americans hate politicians and love their national icons, they tend to assume that the great figures of American history could not have been politicians. For example, they think that Washington never had to do any fundraising, that

Hamilton was not interested in political spin, and that Jefferson was an idealistic statesman. Actually, in 1789 Washington had to borrow $500 from a neighbor to get himself to New York City for his inauguration. Hamilton was a ferocious writer for the press, arguing for his measures and assailing his foes under many pen names. Finally, Jefferson was a master politician by the standards of his era.

Even so, politicians of the early republic differed significantly from politicians today. In Jefferson's era, politicians did not rely on political careers to support themselves. Washington and Jefferson were gentleman-planters living on the labor of slaves (though Washington supplemented that income with land speculations and Jefferson briefly practiced law). Hamilton shuttled between his law practice and posts in government; and it was his law practice that helped to support his family.

Another difference between the founding fathers' era and ours was the amount of time available to politicians then. Jefferson could spend weeks at Monticello while secretary of state, vice president, or president. In the late 1790s, President Adams spent months at a time in Braintree, Massachusetts, caring for his ailing wife. One reason for the languid tempo of the era's politics was the slow speed at which news traveled. Reports of the fall of the Bastille, the execution of Louis XVI, or the signing of the Jay Treaty could take months to reach American shores. Political news within America traveled no faster than a man could run, a horse could gallop, or a ship could sail—giving politicians time to ponder, respond, and decide.

Difficulties of travel and communication also cut down on occasions requiring oratory—as did the era's political culture. Not until the ratifying conventions of 1787–1788 did American lawmaking bodies meet in public view. State legislatures and the Continental and Confederation Congresses met behind closed doors. After the launch of government under the Constitution in 1789, at first only the House held open sessions; the Senate met behind closed doors until an election dispute in 1797 forced a rule change. Politicians rarely had to address an audience. Even at election time, oratory was not a political priority. In Virginia, a candidate's willingness to buy drinks for his neighbors counted more than his ability to win votes by making speeches. Few Americans saw their president, senators, or representatives in person. The twice-yearly circuit court sessions of the early Republic meant that the new government's most visible public faces were those of federal judges.

Modern determinants and landmarks of political authority and influence also did not exist in the early Republic. Under the Articles of Confederation, term limits turned delegates to the Confederation Congress out of office after three years; seniority did not matter in the US Congress until decades after its creation. Instead of regimented political parties, loose, unstable coalitions of shared interests or partisan alliances dominated politics; they could dissolve and recombine with changes in measures or men. Neither state legislatures nor Congress had standing committees with powerful chairmen controlling the legislative agenda. Most committees were ad hoc creations. The procedures governing the Confederation Congress and the US Congress paralleled those used by Parliament and state legislatures.

Politics in this period consisted of groups of politicians working together in legislative chambers and committee rooms, debating, arguing, listening, and seeking to forge consensus, or waiting for the efforts of one man working with paper, ink, and a quill pen. It also meant that politicians had to communicate with the public by means of the written or printed word, explaining policies and influencing the electorate's support of those policies or officials identified with them. Politicians also sought to shape their constituents' perceptions of players of the political game. But the process did not work all one way. Politicians also had to pay close attention to how the people thought. Currents of public opinion often brought unpleasant surprises to those who governed.

Jefferson is a valuable case study in the world of politics in the early Republic. In this system of interactions between governors and the governed, at once complex and rudimentary, he was a master of the game.

The first of Jefferson's political abilities to emerge was his skill with his pen. Adams wrote that Jefferson had "a happy talent for composition" and a "peculiar felicity of expression." Eighteenth-century legislatures did not have legislative assistants, administrative assistants, or staff attorneys at their disposal. If a legislator wanted a bill drafted, he had to do it himself—or find a colleague who would draft it for him. This environment was tailor-made for Jefferson. In every legislative body in which he served, he won the reputation for being a skilled, eloquent draftsman—one reason that he was chosen to draft the Declaration of Independence. Throughout his career, he never used a speechwriter; instead, he did the work himself and consulted with colleagues for advice. In one case, he was not happy with the revision of his handiwork. As late as 1821, he juxtaposed in his *Autobiography* his draft of the Declaration of Independence with the official text, convinced that any reasonable reader would prefer his version.

In one case, President Jefferson was willing to accommodate revisions suggested by others. In October 1801, the Baptists of Danbury, Connecticut, sent him a frantic appeal for support in their battle with a hostile Federalist and Congregationalist majority. Jefferson prepared and circulated to his cabinet a draft response to their letter; he paid close attention to the views of Postmaster General Gideon Granger and Attorney General Levi Lincoln, New Englanders who knew their region and its politics well. Then he revised his letter, which he sent on January 1, 1802. As a statement of his constitutional principles, it gave the

Danbury Baptists the moral support they sought without committing his administration to action on their behalf.

Throughout his career, Jefferson sought to order the world with words. Not just in his time, but in the span of years from his time to ours, Americans have argued about the character of America, the nature and destiny of the American republic, the shape of the good society, relations between church and state, and the meaning of liberty and equality, within the intellectual matrix established by his words. As Abraham Lincoln wrote in 1859, "the principles of Jefferson are the definitions and axioms of free society."

Jefferson's political mastery went beyond draftsmanship. Politics is a matter of the human equation as much as it is one of finding the words to express political principles. Eighteenth-century politics was a face-to-face affair; thus, such personal qualities as affability, a willingness to listen and to appear to listen, an ability to hold one's tongue, and a gift for forging personal relationships were integral to political success. Jefferson had these skills in ample measure. In Virginia's House of Burgesses and in the Second Continental Congress, he won colleagues' trust and respect. In dealing with members of the House and the Senate while he was secretary of state, he drew on skills he had honed in five years of representing the United States in France. And one of his greatest achievements as president was his deft management of the pro-administration majorities in Congress.

The elderly John Adams suggested another reason for Jefferson's success. Writing to Benjamin Rush, Adams reflected on the great men he had known. With insight, envy, and resentment, he noted that Washington, Franklin, and Jefferson all had a gift integral to their reputation as great men, a gift that neither Adams nor Rush had: the gift of silence. Adams complained that the ability to keep silent gave the person possessing that gift a false reputation for profundity; others would fill the silence with deep meanings that he might not have intended. Jefferson knew when to keep his mouth shut, and he used that knowledge to great advantage.

Jefferson hated confrontation. For this reason, in a trait that he developed perhaps to extreme lengths, he crafted a series of public faces to show to those whose support he wanted to win or whose opposition he wanted to blunt. His purpose was to persuade the person sitting opposite him that he agreed with that person or was willing to accept that person's views. By the end of a conversation, anyone sitting across the table from Jefferson, unless naturally suspicious, would be convinced that Jefferson was on his side and grateful for that support. Even with a suspicious person, Jefferson would use every last iota of his conversational brilliance, learning, and collegiality to fend off confrontation.

No politician can escape confrontation altogether. In cabinet meetings in Washington's administration, when Hamilton orated as if addressing a jury, Jefferson would sit silent, puncturing the flow of Hamilton's words with a sarcastic comment. When confrontation seemed unavoidable, Jefferson would stage a tactical or strategic withdrawal; in late 1793, for example, he resigned as secretary of state and returned to Monticello—a pattern recurring throughout his life.

Jefferson was an astute student of public opinion. In his time, ideas, information, and gossip passed between elite politicians and from elite politicians to the general public and back again through middlemen. For example, Madison's friend in Virginia, George Lee Turberville, sent him letters packed with political information about politics back home; in return, Madison sent him letters detailing politics in the center of American public life. So, too, Madison served as Jefferson's chief informant and his most trusted advisor. Similarly, Abigail Adams was her husband's chief advisor and political informant, though John Adams had friends in Massachusetts who also sent him news from home.

What news passed between these circles of friends and allies? One kind of news had to do with the substance of political measures. A second kind had to do with who was allied with or opposed to whom, who was in and who was out, who had power and influence and who did not. A third kind enabled the recipient to form a clear picture of a politician's character. Did he walk or ride his own horse? Was he drawn in a carriage? If so, how many horses drew the carriage? Did he powder his hair or not? Did he wear ostentatious clothing or plain, simple republican garb? Did he bow or shake hands? It was best to conduct oneself in as plain, simple, and republican a manner as possible; ostentation was a sign of leanings to aristocracy or even to monarchy.

Washington and Jefferson paid close attention to the politics of self-presentation. When Washington arrived at his inauguration in New York City on April 30, 1789, he wore a plain brown woolen suit of American manufacture. His choice of attire said three important things—he took office not as General Washington but as George Washington, Esq., a civilian; he took office as a committed republican; and all should buy American, as he did. Similarly, when writing in his diary on May 24, 1790, Senator William Maclay of Pennsylvania described Secretary of State Jefferson's testimony before a Senate committee; he noted that Jefferson's clothing seemed rumpled and not quite tailored to fit, and that Jefferson lounged in his seat. Jefferson dressed and carried himself as a silent republican reproach to monarchic or aristocratic fashions or habits. Fashions and habits were symptoms of underlying social and political ailments afflicting a republic—or of social and political views that can cure those ailments.

Sometimes the way a politician dressed or behaved could be misread. Vice President John Adams, criticized for his opulent attire, complained that he was wearing the only clothes he had (those from his time as American minister in Britain) because he could not afford a new wardrobe. Because he had to wear old fine clothing instead of spending money he did not have to buy plain new clothing, he got the unfair reputation of being aristocratic when he was being economical.

Political gossip also focused on such things as toasts offered at banquets, or who conversed with whom and about what; it was the raw material that politicians and citizens used to assess those aspiring to leading roles in the nation's public life. Knowing that gossip helped to shape the public character and reputation of those who would lead the nation, politicians had to ensure that their characters were worthy—and tried to show that their foes' characters were not.

In the intricate grammar of political combat prevailing in the early Republic, Jefferson was an expert. He collected rumors, anecdotes, and gossip—scribbling them on scraps of paper within minutes of hearing them. Eventually, he gathered these scraps into "three volumes bound in marbled paper"—an account that he hoped would present a true history of the early republic's political life, challenging the Federalist version in Chief Justice John Marshall's *Life of George Washington*. Juxtaposing official opinions and memoranda with gossip, Jefferson wanted his readers to understand that American politics was operating on two levels; at the hidden level of gossip was the real story of a titanic struggle for the soul of the United States. In a political world lacking formal determinants of status, leadership, affiliation, and allegiance, the key variable of politics was the character of the individual politician; shaping how character is perceived became a vital political battleground. Jefferson was brilliant at keeping track of how characters were or ought to be perceived, and at working with those who thought as he did to encourage proper perceptions among the people.

Jefferson also was adept at guiding himself by the values governing American politics. One value was the perception of political ambition as dangerous. One should not seem to want power; one should accept power only with reluctance, yearning for the chance to lay the burden aside and to return home. Washington presented himself this way throughout his career. When the Second Continental Congress convened in early 1775, Washington arrived as a Virginia delegate wearing his old uniform as a colonel of the Virginia militia—reminding the other delegates that he had military experience and was ready to serve again should his country need him. But when Congress chose him to be the Continental Army's commander in chief, he bemoaned his lack of qualifications, regretted the need to accept his appointment, and began his yearning for retirement, which he kept up in public and private for eight years. He meant it—but he knew that it was vital for him to be seen and heard meaning it.

So, too, Jefferson expressed reluctance to assume the burdens of office, yearned for retirement, expressed his unhappiness in public life, and invoked his desire to return to his family, his plantation, and his books. Again, he meant every word of it, but he knew that it was vital to his success as an elite national politician to be seen and heard meaning it. Like Washington, Jefferson had a stern sense of the public good and a conviction that if he could further the public good by assuming office, duty and civic virtue required him to do so. Jefferson had an ideological reason beyond his sense of the public good. He had a vision of the good society, and he was convinced not only that his was the proper vision of the good society but that he was the best man to help his country achieve that vision. Jefferson's ambition was not just or mostly for himself. Rather, he sought to win authority to vindicate his vision of the good society.

Jefferson's vision of a good society emerged from the Declaration of Independence, from his revision of Virginia's laws, from *Notes on the State of Virginia*, from his inaugural addresses and presidential messages, and from his letters. Its basis was a society devoted to agriculture practiced by a nation of yeoman farmers; cities, trade, and commerce were necessary evils. His watchwords were republican simplicity and virtue, insulated from corruption that would bring aristocracy and monarchy. Religion also should be pure, republican, free, not coerced by government or religious hierarchy, purged of the corruptions imposed by priestcraft.

One pivotal element of Jefferson's vision of a good society is its contrast with another vision of society that haunted him. The specter preoccupying Jefferson was what he confronted in 1784 when he arrived in Europe to begin his service as an American diplomat. He lived in France, with visits to Britain, Italy, the Netherlands, and the German Rhineland. During his travels, he took notes of life in these nations, and he wrote home about his impressions. The strongest theme of his letters about Europe is his horror at corruption, decadence, and waste, which monarchy inflicted on great nations—particularly in France.

Driving these impressions was Jefferson's belief that monarchic and aristocratic corruption in Britain had led to the corruption of British liberty and to its attempts to undermine liberty in America. Jefferson's travels intensified his views. He believed that similar corruption had brought down the Roman Republic, leading to the tyranny of the Caesars. As a result, when in 1789 Jefferson returned to the United States, he was ready to see anything echoing European corruption as a harbinger of American corruption, which he opposed with all his might.

These preoccupations help explain what some scholars dismiss as Jeffersonian fanaticism. Jefferson held his views strongly, applying them with cookie-cutter rigidity to what he saw in America. Hamilton's fiscal policy reminded him of the policies of Sir Robert Walpole, with their corrupt undermining of English liberty. Hamilton's design to strengthen the executive branch reminded him of monarchic corruption in Britain and France, and the dangers to liberty and democracy that those measures posed. Using a standing army to suppress domestic revolt, as Washington and Hamilton did in 1794 against the Whiskey Rebellion in western Pennsylvania, seemed to Jefferson another step in bringing tyranny to America.

President Jefferson practiced a republican politics of self-presentation, of collecting and disseminating the right forms of political intelligence, and of using well-chosen words to order the world. Hating speechmaking, he ended the practice of delivering a yearly presidential address on the state of the Union before a joint session of Congress. This decision spared him an annual public ordeal; more important, it abolished a quasi-monarchical practice (echoing the British "speech from the throne" that opened sessions of Parliament) as having no place in the United States. He used letters to inform the public of his views, knowing that a letter from a political leader on a great public question would soon become public. By contrast, many of his private letters warned their recipients not to share them, for he knew that a letter from his pen, unless safeguarded from public view, would not stay private for long.

He used customs of dress and etiquette in the same way. His "pêle-mêle" seating at presidential dinners, with people choosing their own seats, challenged the European custom of seating people according to their status. So, too, when in 1803 he received the British ambassador Sir Anthony Merry wearing a dressing-gown and carpet slippers, he was rejecting quasi-monarchic diplomatic ceremonies and customs, which he abhorred as threats to republican virtue.

Jefferson said that he hated being president, calling the office a "splendid misery," and he meant it. Serving two terms, he chose not to seek a third. Retiring to Monticello, he never left Virginia again. Even so, he remained a public figure, and he took pains to shape a new role for himself—that of ex-president.

Washington, unique in American public life, was the American Cincinnatus, who had made a profession of setting aside executive power and returning to the ranks of the people out of his own inclination and out of a sense of duty to the republic; his retirement did not make him an ex-president because he was more than that. Because John Adams had been defeated at the polls when he sought a second term, and because he was so wounded by what he deemed an unjust rejection at the people's hands, he withdrew into himself for years after his defeat, not reemerging into public life until the close of Jefferson's presidency. Jefferson was the first man to choose to assume the role of an ex-president and to shape that role.

Even Jefferson's role in his later years—the sage of Monticello—had a political cast. In his letters, he sought to influence American cultural, scientific, intellectual, and political development—fostering principles close to his heart, encouraging the writing of American history and biography, and collecting and preserving primary sources. His retirement project took up a cause that he had cherished for decades—educational reform. As a discontented alumnus of the College of William and Mary and as an exponent of an enlightened citizenry as a bulwark of a democratic republic, he founded a new kind of university, allied with no religion, welcoming students from everywhere, devoted to the life of the mind. His creation of the University of Virginia—designing the buildings, choosing the faculty, devising the curriculum, assembling lists of textbooks and library books—was a political act as much as anything else in his life.

## Church and state

For centuries, European nations struggled to define the proper relationship between church and state. Did alliances between religion and government bring stability, prevent disastrous contests over religion, or promote religious truth? Would alliances between religion and government produce only bloodshed of the sort that had plagued Europe? All too familiar with the savage record of Europe's religious wars, Americans were determined to guard against similar carnage. One of the founding fathers' proudest achievements was to invent an American solution to these questions. This solution, combining constitutionally protected rights, federalism, and the political temperament needed to recognize that some ambiguities are best left unresolved, was the product of an era of experimentation in church-state relations.

The background for this experimentation is American colonial history. Each of the thirteen colonies was founded at a different time and for different reasons. Some were to be havens of religious liberty for their founders—though not for others who believed differently. Others were business ventures or political experiments in which religion was of secondary concern. In all thirteen colonies except Rhode Island, alliances between church and state held sway. One key concern fueling the American Revolution was the worry of some Protestant denominations that the British Crown would make the Church of England the only legitimate church in British North America. Even the Anglican Church's efforts to secure a bishop for the colonies seemed to threaten the legitimacy, even the existence, of non-Anglican churches.

In the early 1770s, defenders of British colonial policy sought to use American religious diversity as a political tool. At the First Continental Congress in 1774, John Jay of New York and John Rutledge of South Carolina argued that the delegates were so religiously diverse that they could not agree on choosing a clergyman to lead them in prayer; how then could they agree on a policy of resistance to Britain? In response, the radical Samuel Adams of Massachusetts proposed that Congress invite the Philadelphia minister Jacob Duché, a conservative Anglican divine, to lead Congress in prayers. Adams's motion defeated Jay's and Rutledge's efforts to deadlock Congress; he knew that his proposal would persuade other delegates that the Massachusetts men were reasonable colleagues with reasonable grievances deserving a fair hearing. This incident is noteworthy for two points: proving the general recognition of American religious diversity, and showing how politicians could use that religious diversity as a political weapon.

The Revolution not only shattered colonial structures of political authority—it also weakened the Anglican Church's authority in the states. Anglican clergymen who had sided with the Crown and Parliament found it prudent after 1776 to leave America or to make public apologies for their former loyalties. Further, the denominations that had resisted Anglican authority saw opportunities to vindicate their legitimacy and perhaps to claim authority for themselves by allying themselves with state governments. At the same time, more radical denominations such as the Baptists argued that churches were best when they were voluntary, with no ties to the state. Liberal thinkers agreed, embracing separation of church and state.

Modern controversies over issues of church and state give the false impression that only one way of interpreting church-state questions during the founding era is correct. Either the founding fathers intended strict separation of church and state or they intended that government foster the cause of religion as opposed to the cause of atheism. The real history is more complex. Two lines of argument emerged during the Revolution, prevailing in different states and having complementary arguments.

One model of church-state relations, *separationist*, had at its core the principle that religion and the secular realm should be separate. In particular, the state should have no power to coerce religious belief, to force an individual to worship against his or her conscience, or to support religious institutions in which he or she does not believe. This separationist model is codified in Article 16 of the Virginia Declaration of Rights of 1776, which stressed the individual's right to worship in any manner so long as he does so peaceably.

In 1779, as part of his efforts to revise the laws of Virginia, Jefferson drafted a bill for religious freedom. His bill went further than the Declaration of Rights, arguing that because "almighty God hath created the mind free," it was impossible, impious, and illegal to coerce religious belief or observance. Separation of church and state, Jefferson argued, was needed to protect the secular realm and the individual mind from the corrupting alliance of religion and government.

Jefferson's bill languished until Madison revived it in 1785–1786. He acted in response to efforts led by Patrick Henry to secure public funding for "teachers of the Christian religion" (Protestant ministers). Opposing Henry's efforts, Madison framed his "Memorial and Remonstrance Against Religious Assessments," recognized as the greatest presentation of the case for separation of church and state. On religious freedom, Madison agreed with Jefferson, but in the "Memorial and Remonstrance" he added a vital element to the argument—that any alliance between religion and government also would threaten the purity of religion, exposing it to the corrupting influences of the secular world and government power. Madison structured his argument as a triangle of mutually supporting principles, echoing those of Roger Williams, the seventeenth-century Puritan religious thinker who founded Rhode Island.

In a titanic struggle, Madison defeated Henry's bill; then he revived Jefferson's bill on religious freedom and rammed it through the state legislature. When the news reached Jefferson in Paris, he publicized it. Word of the Virginia Statute for Religious Freedom spread through Europe, winning acclaim for Jefferson and Madison as enlightened statesmen.

The Virginia experience and the ideas of Jefferson and Madison do not distill the American people's views on church-state relations. Other states followed a different model. This *nonpreferentialist* or *accommodationist* model taught that an alliance between religion and government was necessary to preserve the people's virtue and morality, which were vital to preserving liberty and republican government. There were two variants of this model. In one (briefly in Virginia and for a time in the Carolinas and some middle Atlantic states), only one denomination of Protestant Christianity, the Episcopal (formerly Anglican) Church, was *established* as the state's official religion receiving tax support for ministers and church buildings. *Dissenting* sects—sects other than that established by law—could worship but could not receive state support for ministers or churches. The other variant, prevailing in New England states (except Rhode Island), created *multiple establishments*; several denominations of Protestant Christianity were established by law and entitled to receive public funds for their support.

These two models of church-state relations coexisted in the states from the 1780s through the 1830s. Gradually, states with establishments abolished them, by statute or by revising state constitutions. By 1833, when Massachusetts abolished its multiple religious establishment, the American people had embraced separationism. Even so, some states kept religious tests for voting and holding office, benefiting members of favored religions and excluding members of disfavored religions. Pennsylvania, for example, required any candidate to swear to or affirm his belief in the divine inspiration of the Old and New Testaments. The American consensus on church-state relations shifted to a generally separationist model within a religious consensus informed by Protestant Christianity.

Some scholars suggest that the founding fathers were more willing to accept diversity of religious belief and more skeptical of alliances between religion and government than most Americans were. This assumption overlooks founding fathers with conservative religious views. Further, the founding fathers' struggles with issues of church and state teach two lessons. First, they were engaged with their countrymen in a great experiment. Second, this experiment was the product of a creative argument between leaders and people taking place in all thirteen states and requiring decades to achieve final results.

Even after the last religious establishment's fall, Americans argued about religion's proper role in American public life. Two issues kept the argument alive. First, Americans created new institutions, such as public schools, where controversy over church-state relations focused. Second, American religious diversity expanded due to immigration and the explosion of denominationalism. To this day, issues of church-state relations rage in American politics and law; both sides invoke the founding fathers to support their views.

## Equality

Posterity judges the founding fathers most harshly on the issue of equality. Despite the proclamation of the Declaration of Independence, "We hold these truths to be self-evident, that all men are created equal," the Revolution left many issues of equality unaddressed. The founding fathers grappled with conflicting ideas about equality—but sometimes avoided the issue altogether. Washington, for example, had to overcome his exasperation with New England soldiers who elected their own officers and refused to abide by hierarchical military discipline. John Adams had to contend with his wife Abigail's eloquent plea that the new nation's constitution-makers and lawmakers "remember the Ladies" while devising institutions and laws for an independent America. In the 1780s, in his only book, *Notes on the State of Virginia*, Jefferson sought to justify slavery by making conflicted arguments for the inferiority of those of African descent, while conceding slavery's monstrous injustice.

The most serious of all issues of equality confronting the founding fathers was slavery. By the eighteenth century, slavery was present throughout British North America and Britain's Caribbean possessions. Slavery had become essential to the southern colonies' agricultural economies—tobacco and wheat in Virginia and North Carolina and rice and indigo in South Carolina and Georgia—but slavery was recognized and protected by statute from New England to Georgia.

The Revolution's rhetoric of liberty and equality spurred Americans in some states to reassess slavery and to ask whether it was consistent with arguments for liberty. Some younger politicians and military men, such as Colonel John Laurens of South Carolina, argued that the states should recruit slaves for their militias, promising them freedom if they would fight for the American cause—but most politicians rejected Laurens's views. Similarly, British officers promised freedom to slaves who would desert their owners and enlist in British units—but these promises were a tactic to undermine American resistance rather than expressions of anti-slavery principles; British forces did little to honor their promises to slaves who accepted the offer. In 1781, in one of the war's most horrifying episodes, the British army besieged at Yorktown decided that they could not share supplies with the runaway slaves (and their families) flocking to British lines. They drove these refugees into the "no man's land" between the armies. Artillery fire slaughtered the runaways.

Even after the war's end, the states were slow to act on slavery. In 1780, Pennsylvania enacted a gradual-emancipation statute freeing people of African descent born after the law's enactment, but only after they had reached twenty-eight years of age. Pennsylvania did not end slavery until 1847. In 1783, a series of lawsuits known as the "Quock Walker" case ended when Chief Justice William Cushing of the Massachusetts Supreme Judicial Court held that, under the state's 1780 constitution, slavery could not exist legally in the state. In 1799, New York enacted a gradual-emancipation statute like Pennsylvania's, with slavery ending in 1827. These states acted not necessarily because of devotion to liberty and equality but because slavery had acquired diminishing importance to their economies. In states where owning slaves and using slaves to farm were economic factors, slavery was entrenched by law and public opinion.

The Revolution raised new questions about slavery and the status of African Americans. As contrasts between the ideology of liberty and the reality of slavery sharpened, more Americans began to dislike and denounce slavery. Nonetheless, during the founding era, tough-minded, determined resistance by those with a stake in slavery overcame the majority's widespread but mild anti-slavery sentiment. Advocacy of abolition (using government power to abolish slavery) was a minority viewpoint in the early Republic, though anti-slavery sentiment existed, mostly in northern states.

The most controversial example of the founding fathers' failure to confront slavery is the making of the Constitution. The Virginia Plan, proposed by the Virginia and Pennsylvania delegations as the basis for the Convention's work, used a system of proportional representation based on each state's number of free inhabitants. On June 13, 1787, an amendment added a clause including the words "three-fifths" of "other persons," a euphemism for slaves. This three-fifths clause found its way into the Connecticut Compromise on representation and taxation that became a core component of the Constitution. The Constitution's system of representation gave southern states extra weight in the House and in the Electoral College, entrenching slavery—though without using the word.

The slavery question arose again in August 1787. Delegates from slave states in the Deep South, such as South Carolina's Charles C. Pinckney, opposed giving the federal government power to regulate international trade, particularly the slave trade. Though Virginian and other delegates protested, the southerners proved obdurate. They criticized their adversaries as hypocrites, arguing that a ban on importing slaves from overseas closed the slave market to all suppliers of slaves except Virginia, a slave-producing state that would willingly supply the needs of consumers of slaves, shipping them on New England vessels. The southerners secured a compromise barring the federal government from banning the overseas slave trade for twenty years, but allowing limited taxation of imported slaves. In return, the South Carolinians conceded that Congress could enact general laws regulating foreign trade by a simple majority. Another part of this compromise on slavery was a clause added to the Constitution, from the 1787 Northwest Ordinance, providing that a fugitive slave fleeing a master across state lines could be captured and returned to his master.

Convention delegates knew the southern states' commitment to slavery; they believed pro-slavery delegates' threats that South Carolina, North Carolina, and Georgia would leave the Convention unless the Constitution protected slavery. In a choice between striking a blow against slavery and holding the Union together, the Convention chose to preserve the Union.

At the same time, recognizing growing anti-slavery sentiment, the framers omitted the words "slavery" and "slaves" from the Constitution. On August 22, 1787, Elbridge Gerry of Massachusetts sketched the Convention's approach: "he thought we had nothing to do with the conduct of the States as to Slaves, but ought to be careful not to give any sanctions to it." Adjusting interests of northern and southern states, the delegates gave greatest weight to the goal of framing a Constitution, tiptoeing around issues that would explode their fragile consensus.

This approach to constitution-making, combined with the realities of federalism, also explains why the Constitution is silent about who can vote. Each state had a different way of regulating access to the polls. Because a uniform national standard seemed impossible, the Convention left suffrage to the states. In 1870, 1919, 1964, and 1971, constitutional amendments imposed limits on what the states can do about access to the polls—barring discrimination based on race, sex, nonpayment of a poll tax, and age (eighteen and over). Even these amendments leave undisturbed the Convention's decision to leave voting to the states.

# America in the world

The United States of America began as a fragile confederation of former colonies on the fringes of the Western world, regarded by European powers as at best a distraction and at worst an annoyance. Rich in natural resources yet plagued by enduring problems of governance, the United States was adrift in great-power politics. The founding fathers also faced Native American nations with whom they coexisted in uneasy peace punctuated by bitter wars.

Independence gave Americans added reason to worry about the world. Because they were no longer under British rule, they could not look to Britain for protection. In response, such founding fathers as Adams and Hamilton urged a neutral stance toward Europe, though seeking commercial opportunities with European nations; they worried about European wars' effects on America. Others, such as Jefferson, argued that because a great ocean separated Europe and America, the United States could turn its back on the Old World.

Spending time in Europe had various effects on Americans, shaping their views on foreign policy. Franklin had crossed the Atlantic several times and had lived in Britain for nearly two decades; he was more seasoned and urbane regarding Europe than were his younger colleagues Adams, Jay, and Jefferson. Franklin took Europe in stride and made gentle but pointed fun of Europeans' pretentiousness.

By contrast, Jefferson and Adams were traumatized by their years in Europe. Jefferson loved European literature, music, and architecture; in some ways, his time in Europe was one of the happiest of his life. Still, he hated European decadence, and he was aghast at the exploitation and corruption that he saw in France. In letters, he argued that a great nation was letting itself be destroyed by the evils of monarchy, aristocracy, and an established church, all exploiting and oppressing the people.

His vehement support of the French Revolution and his casual acceptance of its horrors flowed from his view of the old regime. Seeing America and Europe as equals, he concluded that America had more to teach Europe than Europe had to teach America.

Unlike Jefferson, Adams came to Europe as a provincial, making the difficult journey from his farm in Braintree to the center of the Western world. Awed and disgusted by what he found there, Adams felt inner conflicts about European manners, politics, and customs. Adams (unlike Jefferson) had almost no interest in European art or architecture. And yet he disliked Old World snobbery as much as Jefferson did, but he also wondered whether Europeans were right about American provincialism—and he suspected that they were right about his own.

These experiences jarred both men out of sync with things in America. On his return, Jefferson found his countrymen entranced by trade, commerce, and luxury goods, eager to embrace fiscal policies and hierarchical and deferential customs. To him, such things were symptoms of incipient monarchy and aristocracy, the political equivalent of the plague; he responded with all the vehemence, eloquence, and horror of which his humorless, thin-skinned soul was capable. Adams found his countrymen entranced by something different—fantasies of democratic revolution fueled by the French Revolution. He was terrified by the optimism with which so many Americans welcomed the turbulence convulsing France and by the democratic heresies he associated with Franklin, Paine, and Jefferson. Where Jefferson feared the rise of an American monarchy and aristocracy, Adams feared the emergence of a vengeful American mob seeking to destroy good order.

Most Americans had little or no experience of Europe. Even so, they realized that European upheavals could embroil America. For these reasons, America's place in the world gave new importance to key issues of constitutional design having no precedent in state constitutions or the Articles of Confederation. Who would control foreign relations and issues of war and peace?

Aware of the Confederation's weaknesses in world affairs, the delegates to the Federal Convention gave priority in designing the Constitution to giving the new government power to defend American interests in that hostile world. Therefore, they balanced the need for creating a vigorous, flexible, and effective executive with their commitment to republican government and their suspicions of executive power.

The obvious model was the unwritten British constitution, which gave the king control over war, peace, and foreign relations. Such matters seemed suited to executive power, yet the delegates did not want to recreate an elective version of the British Crown. For this reason, they listened to but rejected out of hand Hamilton's proposal that a single chief executive, indirectly elected to serve during good behavior, hold principal power over issues of war, peace, and diplomacy.

The Constitution created an innovative chief executive, the presidency, and what the eminent political scientist Edward S. Corwin called an "invitation to struggle" between Congress and the president. It made the president commander in chief of the nation's armed forces, but Congress had power to declare war, though some delegates noted that the president could repel sudden attacks. It gave shared power and responsibility for treaty-making to the president and the Senate: the president might negotiate a treaty, but the Senate had to ratify it by a two-thirds vote.

The Constitution left unclear what independent authority the president had over foreign relations. As a result, when in 1793 the United States had to decide whether to remain neutral in the war between Revolutionary France and conservative European monarchies led by Britain or to honor its 1778 alliance with

France, President Washington and his cabinet concluded (with Jefferson dissenting) that the president had independent authority to decide the question and to issue a proclamation of neutrality having the force of law. In 1798, facing a crisis in relations with France, President Adams worked with a Federalist majority in Congress to rescind American treaties with France and to authorize American naval vessels to attack French vessels. By 1800, Adams decided that a war with France was unnecessary and undesirable; he invoked his independent authority to send a diplomatic mission to end hostilities with France, despite opposition from Federalists in his cabinet. As a result, Adams forced Secretary of War James McHenry to resign and, when Secretary of State Timothy Pickering refused to resign, fired him. These acts established precedents supporting presidential authority to remove executive branch officials.

President Jefferson's efforts to use presidential power creatively and effectively resulted in an unusually successful first term. His two great accomplishments were acquiring Louisiana from France and sending the Lewis and Clark expedition to survey the territory, encouraging scientific inquiry while projecting American military power into the heart of North America. Jefferson's second term was more troubled and disappointing. His efforts to compel the warring powers of Britain and France to cease hostilities by cutting off trade with them failed; his Embargo damaged the American economy more than it hurt Britain or France. And when President James Madison asked Congress to declare war against Great Britain in 1812 because of British attacks on American shipping, the war was an embarrassment for American arms until the unexpected victory in 1815 of General Andrew Jackson and his small army over a larger British army at New Orleans.

By 1815, the Constitution's arrangements for dealing with issues of war and peace had prevailed, with the presidency having established an independent role for itself. Two clusters of factors explain this result. First, as Alexander Hamilton argued in *The Federalist* No. 70, a single chief executive brings the valuable qualities of "decision, activity, secrecy, and dispatch" to exercises of executive power; these qualities are peculiarly applicable to diplomacy, war, and peace. Second, the part-time nature of American government in this period helped to elevate the presidency. Congress was not in constant session whereas the president or key members of the executive branch nearly always were available to meet whatever foreign crisis arose. Further, the slow pace of events allowed more time for debate—a practice usually associated with Congress. In theory and in fact, the early national period created fewer opportunities for a free-wheeling president and more opportunity for executive-legislative cooperation and consultation and shared action.

## The Constitution as exploding cigar

As Jefferson grumbled in 1816, later generations ascribe to the founding fathers "a wisdom more than human" and have treated their handiwork with "sanctimonious reverence." Jefferson recognized that the Constitution is a human artifact that human beings made and that human beings must make work. Because it is a human artifact, it has imperfections. Some of these imperfections were compromises pitting the struggle to create the best possible constitution against the effort to create a constitution that had the best chance of winning adoption. Other imperfections were products of fear, lest attempts to solve such quandaries as slavery or to define a national standard for the right to vote might exacerbate tensions that might destroy the Union and its Constitution. Still others showed that the founding fathers were subject to the same frailties that bedevil human beings in all societies—lapses of creativity or imagination, failures of care or foresight. As John Adams warned his cousin Samuel in 1784, "Our Country, My Friend, is not yet out of Danger. There are great Difficulties in our Constitution and Situation to reconcile Government, Finance, Commerce, and foreign affairs, with our

Liberties.—The Prospect before Us is joyfull, but there are Intricacies in it, which will perplex the wisest Heads and wound the most honest hearts and disturb the coolest and firmest Tempers."

The years between launching the Constitution in 1789 and inaugurating Thomas Jefferson as president in 1801 show that the new Constitution raised problems that its framers and ratifiers did not anticipate or had sought to defer: problems casting disturbing light on some of their cherished ideas, problems causing their expectations and understandings and intentions about the Constitution to blow up in their faces, like an exploding cigar. For example, during the First Congress's first session in 1789, the House of Representatives was writing the legislation creating the executive departments of government—in particular, the departments of state, war, and treasury. Each would be headed by an official with the title of secretary, named by the president with the advice and consent of the Senate. Who should have the power to remove the head of an executive department? The Constitution gives no answer, nor did the debates on framing the Constitution provide guidance.

Four positions emerged from the debates. First, the only way to remove the head of an executive department was impeachment. Second, if the official is named by the president with the advice and consent of the Senate, he should be removed with the advice and consent of the Senate. Third, if Congress devises an office, Congress also can specify in the statute creating that office how to remove the holder of that office. Fourth, as leader of the executive branch, the president has the constitutional power to fire at will the head of an executive department. The House chose the fourth view, which might seem to settle the issue. Yet in a political crisis in 1868 and in cases that the US Supreme Court decided in the 1920s and the 1930s, the matter recurred. In fact, in 1868, the issue led to the impeachment of President Andrew Johnson.

Also in 1789, the Senate confronted the meaning of the phrase "the advice and consent of the Senate." President George Washington, with Secretary of War Henry Knox, came to the Senate, presented his proposed terms for a treaty with the Creek Indians, and asked the senators for their advice and consent. As the Senate's secretary read the terms aloud, with Washington seated in the president's chair and Knox standing by his side, the senators were alarmed and dismayed by what Senator William Maclay of Pennsylvania called his wish "to tread on the Necks of the Senate." Despite Maclay's reverence for Washington, he was determined to maintain the Senate's independence. He asked that Washington leave the proposed terms for the senators to discuss, and that they would send him their response. The senators followed Maclay's lead, and Washington left "in a violent fret," growling, "This defeats every purpose of my coming here." Washington, who had sat through every day of the Convention, held one definition of "advice and consent," but the Senate, six of whose members were framers, had a very different definition in mind.

In September 1789, Congress created the Treasury Department, to be headed by a secretary of the Treasury, with the statutory responsibility to meet requests of Congress to report on the public credit. Congress thought that it was imposing a duty on the secretary of the Treasury, keeping him under their thumb. Instead, Alexander Hamilton, the first secretary of the Treasury, used his duty to write reports on the public credit as the means to set the agenda of American politics, shifting the initiative in policymaking from Congress to the executive branch.

The Electoral College, the mechanism used to choose presidents and vice presidents every four years, had a checkered history before a constitutional amendment altered it in 1804. When the Federal Convention devised the Electoral College, the delegates expected it to thin the herd of candidates; the House would have to pick the president from the top five candidates. George Mason of Virginia predicted that the House would decide nineteen out of twenty elections. It did not work out as he had predicted.

In 1789, the Electoral College made George Washington its unanimous first choice for president, giving the runner-up, John Adams, a plurality of 34 of 69 electoral votes. Federalists rigged this result (persuading electors to scatter their second votes among other contenders while ensuring that Washington received all the first votes) to make sure that Adams could not challenge Washington for primacy. Dismayed by his poor showing, he almost refused to accept election. In 1792, the Electoral College again made Washington its unanimous first choice with 132 electoral votes, with Adams (at 77 votes) doing better than in 1789. In 1796, the first contested presidential election, Adams beat Jefferson by 71 to 68 votes; Jefferson became vice president.

By 1800, the Electoral College had selected the president and vice president three times out of three, without any recourse to the House of Representatives. The election of 1800 was different. When Jefferson and Aaron Burr tied with 73 electoral votes apiece, the result led to the kind of unsettled election that Mason had predicted would happen nineteen times out of twenty. By 1800, however, the people and the politicians had grown so used to the Electoral College picking the president, and the partisan strife dividing Federalists from Republicans had grown so bitter, that the deadlocked 1800 election touched off a major crisis.

As ballot after ballot in the lame-duck House failed to pick a winner, Federalists sought to strike a deal with Burr, who declared his willingness to defer to Jefferson but was insulted by the insistence of Jefferson's backers that he declare himself unworthy to compete with Jefferson for the presidency. Reacting to rumors that the House would strike a deal with Burr or ask Adams to stay in office until the deadlock's resolution, Governor James Monroe of Virginia threatened to march his state's militia on the nation's capital unless the House elected Jefferson. Though Jefferson maintained outward calm, he seethed at what he saw as Burr's treachery. Three weeks before inauguration day, the House chose Jefferson as president on the thirty-sixth ballot, after enough Federalists cast blank ballots to allow Jefferson to be elected by those willing to vote. Within four years, Congress devised and the states ratified the Twelfth Amendment to prevent a repeat of 1800; electors would vote separately for president and vice president.

One final example of a flaw in the Constitution of 1787 almost arose in 1973. Under Article I, section 3, clause 6, the chief justice of the United States presides over the impeachment trial of a president, and the vice president presides over the impeachment trials of federal judges and executive branch officials. Who presides over the impeachment trial of a vice president of the United States? The answer is—the vice president of the United States. The framers of the Constitution may have intended to have the chief justice preside over impeachment trials of presidents *and* vice presidents, having added the vice presidency to the Constitution at the last minute, but they never changed the provision governing who would preside over Senate impeachment trials. In 1973, Vice President Spiro Agnew insisted that his indictment on federal charges of bribery and corruption could not go forward unless and until Congress launched a full impeachment inquiry. Fearing that this process would derail the investigations of charges that President Richard M. Nixon had committed impeachable offenses, House leaders refused to launch an inquiry into Agnew's conduct, deferring to the processes of criminal law. Forced to accept a plea bargain requiring him to resign and to plead *nolo contendere* (no contest), Agnew never got an impeachment trial—let alone the chance to preside over it.

Each of these examples represents a failure of insight or foresight, an instance in which the Constitution's framers fell prey to Robert K. Merton's law of unintended consequences. And each of these examples questions the American tendency to venerate the founding fathers for their omniscience.

This discussion of constitutional exploding cigars suggests that we ought to recognize the founding fathers as human beings who dared greatly and achieved greatly, but who were beset by flaws and failings common to humanity. This nuanced view of the founding fathers not only allows them to step down from the pedestals to which worshipful later generations have elevated them; it also allows later generations to stop abasing themselves before the founding fathers as if they were worshipping idols. The founding fathers' humanity, with complementary human greatness and human frailty, allows us to reclaim our humanity as well.

# Chapter 4

# Legacies: What history has made of the founding fathers

On April 26, 1777, serving in the Continental Congress, juggling committee assignments, and fretting over the war, John Adams wrote to his wife, Abigail. Both Adamses excelled at writing letters—partly by necessity (it was their only way of communicating when he was far away, in Congress or on diplomatic missions) and partly by inclination. Adams used letter writing to ease his soul and to commune with his "dearest friend," his wisest advisor, and staunchest supporter. Pouring out his concerns, ranging from his shaky health to the lack of news from Europe to the failure of Massachusetts soldiers to arrive to replenish Washington's army, he exploded:

> Is it not intollerable, that the opening Spring, which I should enjoy with my Wife and Children upon my little Farm, should pass away, and laugh at me, for labouring, Day after Day, and Month after Month, in a Conclave, Where neither Taste, nor Fancy, nor Reason, nor Passion, nor Appetite can be gratified?

> Posterity! You will never know, how much it cost the present Generation, to preserve your Freedom! I hope you will make a good Use of it. If you do not, I shall repent in Heaven, that I ever took half the Pains to preserve it.

In this passage, Adams spoke for the founding fathers. Posterity haunted them. Would posterity "make a good Use" of the liberties that they had won? Would posterity be grateful to those who had given them those legacies?

It remains hard to disentangle the founding fathers from their achievements—the creation of an independent nation, with a vigorous, adaptable form of government and a body of liberties that, they hoped, would be a model for the world. Because these achievements were products of collective deliberation, we remember the founding fathers as a group—often praised as the most creative and learned gathering of statesmen in history. At the same time, we recognize their limitations and failings, and we struggle to balance gratitude with recrimination in assessing them.

Within this group of nation-builders and constitution-makers, posterity chose individuals to revere or to chastise. The reputations of some founding fathers (George Washington and Benjamin Franklin) have remained consistently high—so high that their mythic images eclipse their humanity. The reputations of others (Thomas Jefferson and Alexander Hamilton) have risen and fallen in historical cycles, suggesting that their struggles with one another when alive continue by proxy long after their deaths. Others (John Adams, James Madison, and John Jay) have languished in neglect, only to be rediscovered and restored to the national pantheon. Tracing these individual threads in the tapestry of American memory illuminates our inconsistent relationship with our past and with the founding fathers.

One battle over the founding fathers has always raged, because so much is at stake—the battle to interpret the US Constitution of the United States and the Bill of Rights by reference to originalism—whether the "original intent," "original understanding," or "original meaning" that we can identify in the founding fathers' words and deeds. This controversy conscripts the past in the service of the present, challenging us to strike a balance between mechanical deference to the founding fathers and equally mechanical rejection of sticking only to the past in solving modern constitutional problems.

## Ancestor worship?

The founding fathers have taken on roles in American life comparable to those assigned to ancestors in cultures such as Confucian China or Republican Rome. Unlike nations with origins lost in the past, the United States began as a political entity in a specific time and place, created by specific individuals. In other words, the United States is a nation because it chose to be; the American people reserve for those who created the nation the roles, functions, and reverence given to biblical patriarchs or patron saints.

What history has made of the founding fathers has unfolded in two ways—one being their developing role in the American people's historical memory, the other being their evolving place in history as interpreted by generations of historians. Increasingly, these tracks have diverged, opening a gap between the public, desiring reassuring narratives presenting role models to guide posterity, and historians, seeking to understand the past on its own terms.

At first, the founding fathers did not realize that they were becoming founding fathers. Rather, opposing tyrannical British measures, they saw themselves as British subjects seeking to defend English rights. They were not interested in independence from Britain; indeed, the British were quicker to charge them with seeking independence than they were to take that step. Not until early 1776, with war under way, did the founding fathers accept that they were founding a nation.

The Revolution helped to fix the idea of founding in American political thinking. As Americans grappled with nation-building and constitution-making, the founding fathers helped to create a national mythology that they hoped would advance political goals. In *The Federalist* No. 2, John Jay reimagined the Federal Convention:

> This Convention, composed of men, who possessed the confidence of the people, and many of whom had become highly distinguished by their patriotism, virtue and wisdom, in times which tried the minds and hearts of men, undertook the arduous task. In the mild season of peace, with minds unoccupied by other subjects, they passed many months in cool uninterrupted and daily consultations, and finally, without having been awed by power, or influenced by any passions except love for their Country, they presented and recommended to the people the plan produced by their joint and very unanimous councils.

The omissions and distortions in Jay's account are clear—he did not mention the delegates who dropped out, walked out, or refused to sign the document, or the disputes that brought the Convention to the brink of dissolution. Jay was not writing history, however. Rather, he sought to evoke a vision of wise founders animated by disinterested patriotism, hoping to persuade his readers to ratify the document that the founding fathers had produced.

This theme persisted throughout the ratification controversy; supporters and opponents of the Constitution told competing stories about its origins and the ideas and motivations of those who framed it. In *The Federalist* No. 37, James Madison outlined the difficulties that the Convention faced in writing a constitution—the range of interests to be accommodated, the novelty and difficulty of the problems confronting the framers, and the challenges presented by using language as a means to order the political world. Madison drew on Franklin's closing speech to the Convention—a rare episode of the gathering's secret debates made public—to show that a perfect Constitution could not be expected from an imperfect gathering. Madison sought to promote a positive image of the framers legitimizing the Constitution and making it palatable to the people.

By contrast, the Constitution's opponents targeted the Constitution rather than the Convention, treating with care the question of criticizing George Washington and Benjamin Franklin. Even Luther Martin of Maryland, an outspoken nonsigning framer, took pains not to assail his former colleagues. In his long published defense of his refusal to sign the Constitution, Martin wrote of the Convention:

> Mr. Speaker, I revere those illustrious personages as much as any man here. No man has a higher sense of the important services they have rendered this country. No member of the convention went there more disposed to pay a deference to their opinions; but I should little have deserved the trust this State reposed in me, if I could have sacrificed its dearest interests to my complaisance for their sentiments.

Martin's attempt to sidestep the Convention's reputation failed. Primed in part by printers and writers who did their work even before the gathering convened, the people were favorably disposed to the Convention, even if they were divided over the Constitution.

The image of unity among the framers was an early victim of the process by which the Constitution became the new nation's form of government. In the 1790s, bitter disagreements broke out over the Constitution's meaning, dividing the founders. Some controversies not only split the founding fathers politically but also tore apart personal friendships. Madison and Hamilton, who had collaborated during the 1780s, each accused the other of betraying his trust. Adams and Jefferson, who had labored together in Congress in the 1770s and as diplomats in the 1780s, parted ways. Madison's political friendship with George Washington was a third casualty. For a time, Madison's gloomy diagnosis in *The Federalist* No. 10 that factionalism was the bane of all republican government threatened to become a prediction of the Constitution's future.

Each side charged the other with having betrayed Revolutionary principles—dramatizing how bitter these divisions had become. The escalating series of attacks and counterattacks culminated in 1800, pitting President Adams, a Federalist, against Vice President Jefferson, a Republican. The election and the bitter dispute over its tie result dramatized just how divisive American politics had become through the 1790s. Once the crisis found resolution with Jefferson's election by the House of Representatives, Jefferson proclaimed his victory a revolution equal to that of 1776, declaring that all Americans—including, by implication, the founding fathers—were reunited in their fealty to principles of republicanism and federalism.

Partisan rancor abated in the nineteenth century's first decades, due in part to the encroachments of mortality on the founding fathers. The survivors, aware that they faced a last battle to define their places in history, sought to leave posterity their version of events, and in many cases, albeit with uneven success, to abandon their old animosities.

This campaign for historical vindication preoccupied John Adams. Though he spent the first years of his involuntary retirement brooding in his home in Quincy, he roused himself in early 1809, beginning a stream of essays for the *Boston Patriot* newspaper that lasted three years. Adams was writing to answer a pamphlet, long forgotten but fresh in his own mind, that Alexander Hamilton had published against him in 1800. A voracious reader, Adams also pored over his friend Mercy Otis Warren's 1805 *Rise, Progress, and Termination of the American Revolution*. Infuriated by Warren's treatment of him, Adams wrote her letter after letter protesting that she had caricatured and misrepresented him. Warren argued back that Adams had given her ample reason to write as she did, but he remained unconvinced.

Having started but left unfinished his *Autobiography*, Adams consoled himself by corresponding with a fellow signer of the Declaration, Benjamin Rush. Both men, who felt cast aside by an ungrateful nation, exchanged eloquent ruminations about the Revolution and their parts in it, each seeking to soothe the other's wounded feelings. How, they wondered, would posterity remember them? Would Americans know the truth about the Revolution? Determined to get his views into the historical record, Adams also answered questions from younger writers hoping to recapture the past; his letters presented colorful, dramatic, and sometimes inaccurate reminiscences of the events he had witnessed.

At Rush's urging, Adams reached out to Jefferson. The letters that they exchanged between January 1, 1812, and their deaths on July 4, 1826, are among the monuments of American literature. That correspondence's recurring themes include the need to educate future generations about the Revolution's origins and course, the credit that its true leading spirits should get, and its meaning for posterity. Though they agreed on how hard recovering the Revolution's history would be, they disagreed on its meaning for the future. Adams never could accept Jefferson's view that the Revolution had launched a great democratic revolution sweeping the globe; he insisted that the Revolution was an American event, with lessons mostly for America rather than for the rest of the world.

Like Adams, Jefferson had been working to set his historical reputation in order; he was as eager and industrious as Adams in his efforts to define the past that he wanted posterity to remember. He answered hundreds of inquiries from biographers and historians, giving vivid reminiscences and valuable biographical sketches of such men as George Washington, Benjamin Franklin, and his beloved mentor George Wythe. Jefferson also wrote an *Autobiography* that got as far as his return to America in 1789. In addition, he prepared a compilation of official papers interwoven with private notes that, he hoped, would present a reliable Republican account of the early Republic.

Jefferson also turned his attention to the visual arts; he advised the artist John Trumbull on painting key scenes from the Revolution. For decades, Trumbull had traveled widely to paint life portraits of as many of the Declaration's signers as possible, hoping to incorporate those likenesses into a grand canvas. Recognizing the power of images, Jefferson offered Trumbull marketing advice, suggesting that the painter commission engravings of his work in a range of grades and prices so that every American home could have a Trumbull hanging on the wall. He also hung one of Trumbull's engravings on the wall of Monticello. (Despite grumbling that Trumbull's painting fictionalized history, Adams displayed a copy of the same engraving on the wall of his home, Peacefield.)

James Madison also arranged his papers for posterity and answered letters asking about the making and proper workings of the Constitution; and about the roles of such men as Jefferson, Washington, and Hamilton. Most important, he oversaw a transcription of his *Notes of Debates in the Federal Convention of 1787*—which, honoring the oath of secrecy sworn by the Convention's delegates in 1787, he kept secret until his death in 1836. He hoped to enlighten readers about the challenges of constitution-making and to provide his widow a source of income from publication rights to his manuscript *Notes*.

Founders no longer available to craft their place in historical memory had relatives, descendants, or friends eager to do the work for them. Hamilton's sons, led by John Church Hamilton, seeking to erect a bulwark against the tides of Jeffersonianism, published a multivolume edition of their father's papers prefixed by an adulatory biography. Similarly, Jefferson's favorite grandson, Thomas Jefferson Randolph, prepared a four-volume edition of Jefferson's writings that sparked furious political controversy when it appeared in 1829—in part because he disclosed Jefferson's private doubts about Washington and other contemporaries.

Chief Justice John Marshall, who revered his commander, wrote the first major life of Washington (1804), abridging it to one volume for use as a textbook. His biography, showing staunch allegiance to the Federalist agenda, spurred Jefferson to prepare his own account of Washington's administration. In 1829, John Quincy Adams began writing a biography of his father as the first step in preparing an edition of the senior Adams's papers; he undertook this project to distract himself after his humiliating defeat by Andrew Jackson in 1828, but in 1830 his election to the House of Representatives opened a new chapter in his political career, forcing him to set the project aside. After Adams died in 1848, his son Charles Francis Adams completed a ten-volume edition of *The Works of John Adams*, including a *Life of John Adams* incorporating the chapters prepared by his father. Senator William Cabell Rives of Virginia, a protégé of Madison, also began a biography of his mentor. Unfortunately, he died before he could complete the work, leaving three massive volumes ending with Madison's retirement from the House in March 1797.

Other writers, noting the American appetite for reading about the nation's formative years and the founding fathers, sought to satisfy that demand. Clergymen Abiel Holmes and Charles Goodrich prepared textbook chronicles of American history, seeking to inculcate patriotism and public service in schoolchildren. A new generation of aspiring historians joined them, hoping to teach lessons about the past to edify posterity. The most industrious was Professor Jared Sparks of Harvard, who became the university's president. Sparks was acclaimed for his editions of the papers of Washington and Franklin, but his aim was adulation; he abridged or destroyed documents that he deemed damaging to his heroes' reputations. He also edited a series of short biographies of American historical figures, the *Library of American Biography*, writing many of the volumes himself.

In the 1820s and 1830s, Americans began to practice ancestor worship. This development was accelerated by the passing of the founding fathers. The result was an increasing tide of anxiety besetting later generations. Those who had created the nation no longer would be present to guide its development. Their deaths closed the heroic age of American history. Those addressing this theme used the words "founders" or "fathers" to describe the men whose lives they were honoring and whose deaths they were mourning.

Washington's death in late 1799 was a catalyst of this process, so it is fitting that in 1800, in this trend's most famous example, Henry Lee delivered a eulogy for Washington (written by John Marshall) dubbing his fellow Virginian "the father of his country." This phrase, which instantly became synonymous with Washington, had deep roots in the Roman Republic, a major inspiration for the founding fathers. Given the abiding popularity of Plutarch's *Lives* as a source of moral exemplars, it was inevitable that Americans would adopt a Plutarchian perspective on the founding fathers—using their lives as a series of moral exemplars supplementing those from the classical past.

The key deaths following Washington's were those of Alexander Hamilton (1804, caused by his duel with Burr), former presidents John Adams and Thomas Jefferson (1826), former president James Monroe (1831), Charles Carroll of Carrollton (the Declaration's last signer, in 1832), Chief Justice John Marshall (1835), and former president James Madison (the Constitution's last framer, in 1836). Some veterans of the Revolution survived into the 1850s, but they were stragglers behind the wave of a major demographic shift.

The most dramatic deaths were those of Adams and Jefferson, both on July 4, 1826, the fiftieth anniversary of Congress's adoption of the Declaration of Independence. Though diehard Federalists grumbled that Jefferson must have taken poison to ensure his death on the fated day, most Americans viewed the matter differently. Orators marked the passing of two great patriots, analogizing their deaths to those of biblical patriarchs and prophets, insisting that these events signaled divine favor for the new nation.

Orators expressed the anxiety of children bereft of their parents. For so long, they mourned, the founders had walked among them, providing sage counsel. The United States had survived the ordeal of the Revolution, the replacement of the Articles of Confederation with the Constitution, the agonizing decade of the 1790s, and the "second War of Independence" in 1812–1815—including the burning of the capital in 1814. Through all those crises, the founders had been there to help the nation weather the storm. What would happen now that they were gone?

Few captured the unease of the generations succeeding the founders better than Abraham Lincoln, who in January 1838 delivered his first major address, "The Perpetuation of Our Political Institutions," before the Young Men's Lyceum of Springfield, Illinois. Lincoln was not quite twenty-nine years old, a lawyer, and an Illinois legislator. Lincoln challenged his audience to preserve the free government created by "a once hardy, brave, and patriotic, but now lamented and departed race of ancestors," whom he dubbed "our fathers." He urged that "reverence for the laws" become "the *civil religion* of the nation," warning against those of "towering genius" who would not be content to preserve the founders' legacy but instead, hungering for eternal fame, would sweep that legacy aside to create one of their own. By contrast, in 1836, the young Ralph Waldo Emerson opened his first book *Nature* with the following lament:

> Our age is retrospective. It builds the sepulchres of the fathers. It writes biographies, histories, and criticism. The foregoing generations beheld God and nature face to face; we, through their eyes. Why should not we also enjoy an original relation to the

universe? Why should not we have a poetry and philosophy of
insight and not of tradition, and a religion by revelation to us,
and not the history of theirs?

On the founding fathers' place in American history, Emerson's
was a minority view, however influential a core text of the
Transcendentalist movement. Lincoln had grasped the spirit
of the times.

Reverence attached to the country's laws, as Lincoln preached, but
it also attached to those who laid the nation's constitutional and
legal groundwork. Recognition that the United States had a defined
origin in historical time made it easier to create a usable past.
Throughout the nineteenth century, commemorations of the nation's

6. In his speeches, Lincoln often focused on the founding fathers
and how to understand and preserve their legacies.

origins—including the fiftieth anniversaries of the Declaration of Independence and the launching of government under the Constitution, and the anniversaries of the births or deaths of such figures as Washington, Franklin, and Jefferson—helped to fix these revered figures in the nation's memory.

Generations lacking direct experience of the founding fathers still had a turbulent relationship with them. That relationship's dominant theme changed from period to period. From the 1820s through the 1850s, anxious veneration reigned; Americans tried to live up to the standards associated with the founding fathers and to heed the warnings they had left for posterity. A disturbing undercurrent of this historical mood was a new contentiousness over which of the nation's great regions, North or South, could rightly claim to be the heir of the founding fathers; this quarrel over that heritage expressed, and accelerated, sectional crisis.

Before and during the Civil War, a tug of war over American historical memory eclipsed anxious veneration. Each side insisted on its fealty to the founding fathers, portraying their adversaries as betrayers of the founders' principles and hopes for the future. Thus, for example, the great seal of the Confederate States of America had at its center George Washington mounted on a horse; the Confederacy's constitution was based on the US Constitution, with alterations making explicit the rebels' understanding of the Union, state sovereignty, and the legitimacy of slavery. By contrast, President Abraham Lincoln insisted that he was defending the experiment in government launched by the founding fathers; in 1863, in the Gettysburg Address, Lincoln tied the Union's cause to the Declaration of Independence and the founding fathers' creation of "a new nation, conceived in liberty and dedicated to the proposition that all men are created equal."

From the end of Reconstruction in 1877 through the early twentieth century, the nation emerged from the shadow of civil war. Relieved at having weathered the ordeal of the Union,

Americans regarded the founding fathers with almost smug veneration. Not only had they overcome the founding fathers' greatest fears—they had solved the problem of slavery, which the founders had left unresolved.

Complacency pervaded the centennials of the Declaration (1876), the Constitution (1887), and Washington's inauguration (1889). Taking the founding fathers and their achievements for granted became so widespread that in 1888 the poet and essayist James Russell Lowell warned that the Constitution was not "a machine that would go of itself."

American views of the founding fathers shifted for another reason. The Civil War became the central episode in American history, representing the failure of the founding fathers' experiment in government, requiring what Lincoln called "a new birth of freedom." That the generation of the Civil War had survived that ordeal while preserving the Union and freeing the slaves eclipsed the founding fathers' achievements. Lincoln's martyrdom at the war's close vaulted him to a posthumous stature equal Washington's. Following 1865, Americans gave Lincoln and Washington equal status as heroes of the American story.

New immigrants to American shores seized opportunities presented by national anniversaries to lay claim to the nation's history. Learning how to be American meant learning and observing the nation's patriotic rituals. The founding fathers became central to this use of American history to instill civic commitments in new immigrants.

In the era of urbanization, industrialization, and immigration that transformed American life in the late nineteenth century, new problems of law and government arose. To what extent could federal or state governments use their lawmaking and regulatory powers to counter economic ills, to enforce safety standards in the nation's factories and workplaces, and to regulate the quality of

7. In 1932, a blimp laid a wreath before the Washington Monument to mark the bicentennial of George Washington's birth—a new application of technology to honoring the founding fathers.

foodstuffs and drugs? Such disputes generated lawsuits; adjudicating these disputes, lawyers and judges invoked the founding fathers as authority to strike down such measures as unconstitutional.

When lawyers and courts used the founding fathers as a collective authority to justify invalidating such measures, they sparked a vehement reaction sweeping into American culture. Political scientists and historians disputed such instrumentalist readings of the nation's past, though their alternative interpretations also conscripted the past in the service of the present. They sought to refute constitutional appeals to the founding fathers and to reconsider the nation's founding.

Charles A. Beard, who began his historical career at Columbia University but became an independent scholar, was the central figure in reconsidering the founding. In *The Supreme Court and the Constitution* (1912), *An Economic Interpretation of the Constitution of the United States* (1913), and *The Economic Origins of Jeffersonian Democracy* (1915), he argued that the founding fathers split along economic and class lines—much like America in his time—and that they were motivated less by disinterested patriotism than by a desire to protect their economic interests. Beard's arguments shaped the assumptions of two generations of historians while fixing the founding fathers at the center of the controversy over interpreting the Constitution. Beard fostered a view of the founding fathers clashing with the veneration prevailing before he wrote, and with arguments of those who still saw them as high-minded patriots.

The disputes over the founding fathers reached their high-water mark in the 1930s, during the presidency of Franklin Delano Roosevelt. An ironic coincidence juxtaposed the constitutional battles of the New Deal with the sesquicentennials of the Constitution's framing and adoption and the launching of government under it. The Roosevelt administration's creative uses of government power (to remedy the damage done by the Great Depression to the economy, to respond to the American people's needs, and to prevent another economic collapse) collided with fierce opposition by conservative politicians and scholars, who insisted that these experiments violated the teachings of the founding fathers. In response, Roosevelt, his supporters, and a host of scholars and journalists reinterpreted the Constitution's origins, stressing the founding fathers' creative experimentation. In one key respect, Roosevelt did not follow the path marked out by Progressive historians who insisted on juxtaposing Jefferson against Hamilton. Rather, he argued (following the Progressive journalist Herbert Croly) that Americans should use Hamiltonian means—a vigorous national government with sweeping economic powers—to achieve Jeffersonian ends—liberty and democracy for the American people.

8. This New Deal–era poster symbolizes the celebration and democratization of the founding fathers, their political examples, and their legacies in the 1930s.

World War II reworked public perceptions of the founding fathers. Confronting Fascism and Nazism spurred Americans to devise a countervailing ideology based on liberty, democracy, and equal rights, rooted in a usable democratic past. The founding fathers became central figures in that ideology, with Jefferson personifying democratic values. In 1943, Roosevelt, who claimed Jefferson as his intellectual hero, dedicated the Jefferson Memorial to mark the bicentennial of the Virginian's birth. Further, Jefferson and Monticello displaced the American Indian and the buffalo on the nickel and Gutzon Borglum carved Jefferson (with Washington, Lincoln, and Theodore Roosevelt) into Mount Rushmore in South Dakota's Black Hills.

During the Cold War's first decades, scholars, politicians, and journalists adapted World War II's American ideology of liberty, democracy, and equal rights to the battle with Communism. The founding fathers remained central to American ideology; complementing that ideology was a brand of history known as "consensus history," stressing areas where historical actors agreed.

For example, Daniel J. Boorstin offered in *The Genius of American Politics* (1958) a celebratory vision of the founding fathers as supreme pragmatists unencumbered by ideology. Their practicality, Boorstin declared, explained why Americans had resisted Marxism's seductive pull. By contrast, Richard Hofstadter, in *The American Political Tradition: And the Men Who Made It* (1948), presented a cool, ironic reading of American history criticizing its constricted vision of politics and its failure to consider solutions to enduring national problems falling outside the limits of liberal capitalism. Hofstadter and Boorstin might have disagreed about their views of the consensus uniting the founding fathers—but they would have agreed that the founding fathers remained a crucial part of American history.

At the same time, domestic developments with international implications—the civil rights revolution—shone a bleak light on the founding fathers. In the movement's first stage, focused on defending African Americans' constitutional rights, litigants and judges looked closely at slavery and equality in the time of the founding fathers and during the second founding of the United States, embodied in the Civil War Amendments to the

Constitution. These amendments, forming the Civil War's constitutional settlement, invalidated the compromises on slavery that the founding fathers had built into the Constitution. In the process, those amendments—and renewed judicial interest in them—highlighted the founding fathers' failures to confront slavery.

Historians responding to this changing world transformed study of the Revolution and the Constitution's origins; they probed the compromises at the Constitution's heart. These scholars asked uncomfortable questions—whether the founding fathers had shown a failure of moral nerve, courage, and creativity by accepting compromises over slavery demanded by a southern minority.

Changes in research priorities and methodological categories expanded historians' inquiries into the founding fathers. Social history took center stage—in particular, histories of women, ethnic and racial minorities, Native Americans, and ordinary white Americans falling outside the "political population." These innovations transformed the writing of American history, especially concerning the founding fathers. At its best, this scholarship opened new vistas into the American past and the nation's founding. By expanding the range of historical subjects worthy of study, they supplanted the old narrative of upward progress with a nuanced account acknowledging historical actors' shortcomings measured even by that era's standards.

Other changes in the historical profession reshaped scholarly and popular understandings of the founding fathers and their world—by expanding the range and availability of primary sources. Formerly, researchers had to travel widely to libraries, historical societies, and archives to consult primary sources or had to rely on a narrow range of unsatisfactory published compilations. Documentary editions existed in one of two forms—an early type, sponsored by the federal government or the founder's family, giving modernized texts purged of "embarrassing" or "private" material, and a later type, prepared by a trained scholar commissioned by a major commercial publisher, presenting careful transcriptions of a generous but still inadequate selection from the individual's papers.

In 1950, the launch of *The Papers of Thomas Jefferson* in 1950 began a documentary-editing revolution that transformed American historical scholarship. These editions, prepared by trained historians and published by university presses, present exact transcriptions of the widest possible range of primary sources carefully annotated; they include not just the letters and other documents that the subject prepared but also letters that others wrote to him. Closely related to these "statesman's papers" projects are the "documentary histories"—rigorous editions of all sources relating to events and processes such as the ratification of the Constitution, the first federal elections, the First Federal Congress, and the early years of the Supreme Court and the federal judiciary.

Though requiring decades to complete, these projects have made possible a new depth of research, analysis, and interpretation in examining the nation's past; they also have enriched American literature by rediscovering some of the finest American writing. In particular, these projects have illuminated a complex series of political events integral to the origins of the Constitution yet undeservedly obscure in national memory.

Sometimes a modern edition can rescue a historical figure from the shadows, launching a process of popular rediscovery. Such was the effect of the publication in 1961 by Harvard University Press of the opening installment of *The Adams Papers*, the *Diary and Autobiography of John Adams*. A modern edition can also present a more nuanced picture of a founding father, as with *The Papers of Thomas Jefferson*. Despite the efforts of its founding editor, Julian Boyd, to fix a Jeffersonian vision at its core, the Princeton edition of Jefferson's papers has spawned rich scholarship portraying Jefferson as a sometimes devious, manipulative politician, a deeply conflicted man who shielded himself from conflicts between his views and his conduct.

One byproduct of the documentary-editing revolution was the Broadway musical *1776*, by Sherman Edwards and Peter Stone. *1776* reworks the story of the Second Continental Congress's declaration of independence, featuring John and Abigail Adams, Thomas and Martha Jefferson, and Benjamin Franklin. The play premiered on Broadway in 1969 and ran for three years, winning the Tony award for best musical and spawning a 1971 film version with the original cast. A 1997 revival ran at New York's Roundabout Theatre for nearly a year. (*1776* brought a remarkable number of younger historians into the profession, including the present writer.)

By contrast with the transformative effects of scholarly reconsideration of the founding fathers, official commemorations of bicentennial anniversaries related to the founders uncritically celebrated that history. During the American Revolution's bicentennial, for example, historians were shunted to the sidelines in favor of spectacles—a parade of tall ships in New York harbor and shows of fireworks.

Hoping to avoid a similarly flawed bicentennial for the Constitution, Professor James MacGregor Burns for the American Political Science Association and Professor Richard B. Morris for the American Historical Association founded a joint initiative, Project '87. This initiative's purpose was to encourage scholarly and public discussion of the Constitution, its creation, and its major principles. Unfortunately, the Commission on the Bicentennial of the Constitution, led by former Chief Justice Warren E. Burger, marginalized the scholarly community, preferring celebratory re-enactments of such events as Washington's inauguration.

Historians who re-examined the Revolution and the making of the Constitution continued to ask uncomfortable questions about excluded groups and the failures of the founding fathers' vision. As a publishing counterweight to this historical scholarship, a new genre of historical writing emerged in the 1990s and early 2000s. Dubbed "Founders Chic" by *Newsweek* magazine, these books presented celebratory portraits of founding fathers and the history they helped to make, addressing general readers while brushing aside uncomfortable questions about the founders pursued by academic historians.

Historians and constitutional theorists began to reconsider the centrality of the founding fathers to their own era and to succeeding generations' attempts to understand their past and shape their future. Social history continued to redirect the profession's former preoccupation with "great white men." Growing study of histories of Native American nations and peoples and of free and enslaved African Americans cast the founding fathers in a disturbing light. Some historians take this matter to extremes, spurning as reactionary any attempt to study them. Constitutional theorists, reacting against originalism's growing popularity, lambaste the founding fathers for shortsightedness and failures of creativity.

Other historians have sought to study individual founding fathers within historical and political contexts. These figures thought and acted within a shifting field of expectations by and reactions from the people; they operated in the political realm largely by reference to popular reaction to their policies and conduct. This thoughtful scholarship reconsidering the founding fathers cuts against simplistic veneration.

The man who coined the phrase "founding fathers" gave us sage counsel on such efforts. On May 30, 1922, dedicating the Lincoln Memorial, President Warren G. Harding declared: "Abraham Lincoln was no superman. . . . Lincoln was a very natural human being, with the frailties mixed with the virtues of humanity. There are neither supermen nor demi-gods in the government of kingdoms, empires, or republics. It will be better for our conception of government and its institutions if we will understand this fact."

## Which founding father are you?

On the Internet, we can find websites that ask, "Which Founding Father are you?" They offer questions that you answer to indicate which founding father you resemble. Such websites make a twenty-first-century approach to an enduring question: how do we weigh claims of individual founding fathers to relevance and popularity? Tracing the rise and fall of individual reputations illuminates Americans' relations with their past and what they think that past means.

The most studied example is Thomas Jefferson. From his death in 1826 until the outbreak of the Civil War in 1861, Jefferson was as controversial as he had been in life. Some extolled his commitment to liberty, equality, and the rights of man; some denounced him as the intellectual godfather of nullification, secession, and disunion; and some preferred to extol his state-sovereignty constitutional theory, taking it further than he would have done. From the end of the Civil War in 1865 until the 1920s, Jefferson's reputation fell to its lowest ebb. One reason is the blame that Jefferson got for the Civil War; another reason was that his papers disclosed inconsistencies between his public and private views which, some scholars charged, amounted to dishonesty. From the 1930s through the late 1960s, by contrast, Jefferson achieved apotheosis as a symbol of human rights, religious freedom, separation of church and state, and democratic revolution. Beginning in the late 1960s, however, his reputation again started to fall. Attention to race, slavery, and civil rights and his views on race and African Americans have fostered an ambivalent view of Jefferson. Accelerating this process was the seismic shift of opinion on his relationship with his slave Sally Hemings.

As Jefferson rose, Alexander Hamilton fell, and as Jefferson fell, Hamilton rose. All but forgotten before the Civil War, Hamilton's reputation rose spectacularly in the late nineteenth century, when he was hailed as the father of modern America and the strongest advocate of constitutional Union. The twentieth century's first decades rocketed him to new heights as the most admired founding father after Washington. The New Deal brought a reversal of fortune for Hamilton, stigmatizing him as an apologist for laissez-faire capitalism, wealth, power, and privilege. The Cold War brought renewed appreciation of Hamilton's realism in foreign policy. As Jefferson fell again in the 1990s, Hamilton rose once more, rediscovered as an advocate of national constitutional power; his admirers also contrasted his distaste for slavery (exaggerated into abolitionism) with Jefferson's status as a slaveholder.

Other founding fathers vanished from view or suffered eclipse by contrast with Jefferson and Hamilton. Though venerated between 1836 and 1861 as the greatest of the founders after Washington and Franklin, Madison languished for nearly a century. Following the Civil War, scholars misrepresented him as an advocate of state sovereignty and secession. Though Jefferson's historical stock rose in the 1930s, most treatments of Madison depicted him as Jefferson's protégé, with no independent intellectual status. Not until the 1950s did posterity rediscover Madison as a constitutional theorist. This rediscovery occurred again during the bicentennials of the Constitution and the Bill of Rights.

John Adams's bitter prophecies that posterity would forget him nearly achieved fulfillment. Adams owed this unfortunate fate in part to the tight control that his descendants kept on his papers. Not until 1954, when the family deposited the Adams papers with the Massachusetts Historical Society and agreed to open them to researchers and a modern scholarly edition, did Adams reemerge in the popular imagination—receiving periodic boosts thanks to his becoming an icon of popular culture.

The two gold-standard founding fathers—George Washington and Benjamin Franklin—have long held sway. Even so, public veneration has obscured rather than enhanced comprehension of Washington and Franklin. Here, too, the documentary editing revolution is helping to rebut this tendency, presenting these men in their own words and allowing us to understand them in their full humanity.

Of the first-rank founding fathers, only John Jay still languishes in obscurity. The sources of this neglect are accidents of history—Jay did not sign the Declaration and the Constitution, he wrote only a few *Federalist* essays, and John Marshall overshadowed him as chief justice.

## The dead hand of the past? Originalism

How should we interpret the Constitution? Is there one best way to do so? Because the Constitution originated at a particular time and place as the creation of a specific group of politicians, arguments about the Constitution's origins as the handiwork of the founding fathers came to occupy the core of the process of constitutional interpretation. What did the founders mean? Which founders should we look at to find out what the Constitution means? Should we look the founders at all to find out what it means? These questions have generated a wide-ranging argument over the Constitution's authors, what they intended or understood it to mean, or what an ordinary citizen of that time would have read the document as meaning. The shorthand term for such arguments is "originalism."

No modern constitutional democracy has focused so intensely on originalism as has the United States. In part, the American controversy is rooted in the difference between the origins of the United States and the origins of other nations. It is not just a matter of a specific datable origin for the United States and its form of government—the American nation also was and still is held together by shared constitutional and political values rather than by commonalities of race, ethnicity, or religion. Thus, questions of the nation's origins and purposes are closely bound up with matters of constitutional and political choice. If we are a nation because we chose to be, the next step is to determine what kind of nation we chose to be. That step requires an investigation of what kind of constitution and constitutional system we chose to have at the nation's start, which leads to our choice between deferring to the founding fathers and rejecting their ideas and arguments in light of changing circumstances.

Another question drives the controversy over originalism: does this method of constitutional interpretation restrain judicial discretion, as its backers claim? Proponents of originalism extol it as a bulwark against unelected federal judges, to prevent them from writing their preferences into the nation's law; these judges must be bound by history's commands.

This argument for the jurisprudence of originalism has roots in the ratification controversy's argument over whether a federal judiciary was desirable or dangerous, and in the ongoing disagreement about the roles that federal courts play. It also has roots in constitutional democracy. On this theory, sweeping changes in interpreting the Constitution should come from democratic institutions. If an issue arises requiring a change in constitutional interpretation, that change is best achieved by constitutional amendment, not by unelected and unaccountable judges.

Opponents of originalism reject those arguments. First, instead of certainty and clarity, history supports a wide variety of clashing ways to interpret a constitutional text. Second, these critics argue, judges invoke originalism (a) to reject interpretations that they find too extreme or (b) to avoid blame for interpretations that their critics might find too extreme. Originalism shifts the question from what the constitutional provision means to what a group of dead founding fathers thought it means. Besides questions of political and constitutional principle, evidentiary issues swirl around originalism. Modern originalists use James Madison's *Notes of Debates in the Federal Convention of 1787,* the most comprehensive account available of what the framers said in the Convention. As a Virginia delegate, Madison had a seat enabling him to hear the debates; using his own system of shorthand, he recorded each day's proceedings, spending hours at night transcribing and editing his own shorthand record—though modern researchers have determined that Madison could catch only 5 to 10 percent of what the framers said.

Further, Madison did not think that his notes should be the first resource for interpreting the Constitution. He intended his notes of the framing debates to teach future constitution-makers the challenges of framing a constitution. By contrast, the intent of the Constitution's ratifiers, reflected in surviving records of state ratifying conventions, was his reference point for interpreting the Constitution. Because those delegates were the Constitution's true makers, their intent should be dispositive. Also, state ratifying conventions met in public, arguing for and against the Constitution, airing the arguments for the people.

Madison's argument has two flaws. First, for many years records of the ratifying conventions were scattered, unavailable to researchers until the twentieth century. The rigorous edition, *The Documentary History of the Ratification of the Constitution and the Bill of Rights, 1787–1791,* was launched in the 1960s. Before that edition, scholars had only an incomplete, unreliable edition by Jonathan Elliott (1784–1846), launched in 1827 and reprinted several times over the next few decades. Second, neither the ratifying conventions' records nor the Federal Convention's records were available for research for decades after the Constitution's adoption. Madison's notes were not published until 1840, after half a century of constitutional interpretation. Further, Madison's notes have focused researchers on the convention that produced the Constitution, not the conventions that ratified it—his preferred focus.

Arguments over originalism arose as Americans were setting the new government in motion. The founding fathers and the people divided, often bitterly, over many constitutional and political issues. The Constitution's opponents, resigned to their defeat but determined to continue the battle over the nation's future, criticized the Constitution's supporters for diverging from what they had told the people about what they thought the Constitution meant. These debates may seem abstract after two centuries, but they were severely pragmatic and deadly serious, as such arguments have been ever since the Constitution's framing and adoption.

Two patterns recur in these controversies. First, we see a predictable polarization in arguments about originalism. When originalism favors a specific interpretation of the Constitution, that interpretation's advocates embrace originalism, but when originalism cuts against a given interpretation, that interpretation's advocates reject originalism. Such arguments operate on two levels—on the level of constitutional substance and on the level of praising or rejecting originalism. Second, originalism ends as an interpretative tool for all sides—yielding clashing readings of the historical evidence, generating clashing originalist interpretations of the Constitution. We see such spectrums of historical argument and originalist disputes in such areas as church-state relations and the meaning of the right to keep and bear arms protected by the Second Amendment. Again, however, such arguments about the Constitution take two tracks—that of constitutional substance and that of competing originalisms, seeking to use history to mold law.

Perhaps the most notorious example of originalist argument is Chief Justice Roger B. Taney's opinion in *Dred Scott v. Sandford* (1857). Dred Scott was a slave who sued in federal court to obtain his freedom; his former owner had traveled as an army doctor through the midwestern and western United States with his family and his slaves; in particular, he had lived in free states and in a free territory before returning to the slave state of Missouri. After his owner's death, Scott filed suit for his freedom against his owner's executor, John F. X. Sanford (misspelled as Sandford in the case reports). When the case arrived at the Supreme Court, six justices were ready to reject Scott's lawsuit on the ground that under Missouri law, he could not bring suit in a federal court. (Two other justices were willing to uphold Scott's claim.)

Chief Justice Taney understood the case differently—and hoped to dispose of a divisive political matter by issuing a definitive decision by the Court. He penned a long, seemingly authoritative opinion, which in the eyes of the nation became the opinion for the Court. Taney insisted that the intent of those who framed and adopted the Constitution was dispositive. That intent, he ruled, was that the federal government had no power to limit the spread of slavery. Thus, the long-dead Missouri Compromise of 1820 was unconstitutional, and any attempt to cite it as precedent for congressional power to limit the spread of slavery was also invalid.

The most eloquent and well-reasoned denunciation of Taney's opinion came from Abraham Lincoln. Not only did he contend that Taney was part of a pro-slavery Democratic conspiracy—with former president Franklin Pierce, current president James Buchanan, and Senator Stephen Douglas of Illinois—to fasten slavery on the nation. He also planned a frontal assault on Taney's originalist arguments in *Dred Scott v. Sandford*.

In 1860, hoping to persuade eastern politicians that he was worthy of being the Republican presidential nominee, Lincoln journeyed to New York City to deliver a major address at Cooper Union. Grounding his speech on careful, extensive historical research, Lincoln sought to establish the "original intentions" of "our fathers, who framed the Government under which we live."

He made a powerful case that the founders had welcomed
congressional power to limit the spread of slavery in federal
territories. He used this argument to undermine Taney's
pro-slavery originalist reading of the Constitution; he also
devised a legal-historical argumentative method that has become
a standard in disputes over originalism. If the Court bases its
decision on a reading of history, a skillful, persuasive critique
of that decision's historical basis can undermine the decision's
legitimacy.

The principal consequence of originalist battles has been to raise
questions about the use of originalism. Many constitutional
scholars and historians have coalesced around a position
recognizing the usefulness of originalism as a persuasive factor in
constitutional interpretation but rejecting it as dispositive (that
is, settling a constitutional argument once and for all).

The resurgence of originalism—then called the "jurisprudence of
original intent"—had its beginnings in 1985, when then-attorney
general Edwin Meese III called for a way to anchor freewheeling
judges to the text of the Constitution interpreted solely in the
light of its origins. Meese cited *Dred Scott* to illustrate the
jurisprudential disasters resulting from judges writing their own
preconceptions into the Constitution—despite Chief Justice
Taney's explicit framing of his opinion as an originalist reading of
the Constitution. Paralleling Meese's argument were efforts by
the highly conservative Federalist Society and right-wing legal
academics affiliated with that group to promote originalist
interpretation of the Constitution. The appointments to the
Supreme Court of Justices Antonin Scalia, Clarence Thomas, and
Samuel A. Alito helped to bolster originalism's appeal. Most
recently, Justice Scalia has called for a version of originalism
steering clear of historical inquiries into what specific framers and
ratifiers of the Constitution thought it meant, emphasizing instead
what an ordinary intelligent citizen circa 1787 would read the
Constitution as meaning.

In response, historians have challenged the claims of originalism on grounds of historical methodology. First, originalism does not acknowledge the inadequacies of historical evidence. Second, originalism fails to consider historical and intellectual contexts of the origins of the Constitution and the ways in which those contexts differ significantly from today. Third, in the constitutional system's early years, its workings repeatedly surprised and dismayed those who framed, adopted, or supported the Constitution. Given the Constitution's tendency to diverge from the expectations and understandings of those who framed or adopted it, and given the repeated emergence of problems that the framers and ratifiers never anticipated, it makes no sense to practice rigid fealty to originalism.

Even so, critics of originalism have argued, there is no need to discard inquiries into the Constitution's origins as a means to assist modern interpretation of the document. First, the framers and ratifiers were "present at the creation"; their debates and arguments have much of value to teach us about constitutional creation and creative adaptation, both shaping the origins of the Constitution. Second, because the founding fathers were among the most learned and profound political and constitutional thinkers that this nation has produced, we need not sacrifice their arguments' persuasive value even if we reject the binding force of originalism. We ought to treat their wisdom as a resource on which to draw in solving puzzles posed by the operations of the Constitution and by attempts to apply its principles and provisions to new problems and controversies. At the same time, though we may want to start with the founding fathers, we should not stop there—and they themselves would counsel us not to stop there.

Ordering the world with words is the essence of politics as the founding fathers learned and practiced it. We still have much to learn from them about politics—and about how to order the world with words.

# Epilogue: The founding fathers, history, and us

Americans' contentious relationship with the founding fathers has unfolded within and been shaped by two linked questions. How much do the founding fathers resemble us and how much do they differ from us? To what extent must we keep faith with them, and to what extent must we challenge them or set them aside in the face of changing conditions and problems? That the American people still govern themselves under a written constitution largely framed by the founding fathers gives these questions urgency.

The Preamble's statement that the Constitution's primary purpose is "to form a more perfect Union" offers a way to answer these questions. The phrase "a more perfect Union" suggests the framers' recognition that the Constitution not only was improving the Union as defined by the Articles of Confederation but that both it and the Union were capable of further improvement. During the ratification controversy, supporters of the Constitution invoked the amending process codified in its Article V as a means to repair defects in the Constitution. Given this remedy, the Constitution's backers described the choice before the American people as between the hope of future good and no hope at all.

The idea of perfecting the Union has been a vital feature of American constitutional culture. In particular, that idea has been a key theme of African American constitutional thought. African

American activists, orators, politicians, and jurists, all of whom have played essential roles in the American constitutional experiment, offer revealing variations and developments of this theme, illuminating the complex relationship between the founding fathers and posterity. All sought to engage with the founding fathers; all blended clear-eyed criticism of their greatest failures with hopeful invocations of their principles as means to set those failures right—to perfect the Union. Given the centrality of the African American experience to American history, the pattern of thought traced by these thinkers has urgent relevance for Americans' evolving relationship with the founding fathers.

On July 5, 1852, Frederick Douglass gave an Independence Day address to more than five hundred abolitionists in Corinthian Hall in Rochester, New York. Douglass had already won international fame with his 1845 *Narrative of the Life of Frederick Douglass* and lectures on slavery, abolition, and emancipation. Thirty-four years old, tall, and strongly built, with a powerful voice and a mesmerizing delivery, Douglass was a rising star of the national abolitionist movement. Standing at the podium, he did not mince words for his genteel audience:

> What to the American slave is your Fourth of July? I answer, a day that reveals to him, more than all other days in the year, the gross injustice and cruelty to which he is the constant victim. To him, your celebration is a sham; your boasted liberty, an unholy license; your national greatness, swelling vanity; your sounds of rejoicing are empty and heartless; your denunciations of tyrants, brass-fronted impudence; your shouts of liberty and equality, hollow mockery; your prayers and hymns, your sermons and thanksgivings, with all your religious parade and solemnity, are to him mere bombast, fraud, deception, impiety, and hypocrisy—a thin veil to cover up crimes which would disgrace a nation of savages. There is not a nation on the earth guilty of practices more shocking and bloody, than are the people of these United States, at this very hour.

This passage introduced the best-remembered feature of Douglass's address, his indictment of American hypocrisy in the face of slavery's conflict with celebrations of American freedom.

Unlike so many in the abolitionist movement, Douglass refused to fix the blame for slavery on the founding fathers. Instead, he argued that they were the victims of gross misrepresentation by his era's defenders of slavery: "*It is a slander upon their memory,* at least, so I believe." Insisting that the Constitution was a "GLORIOUS LIBERTY DOCUMENT," Douglass argued that the Constitution's text nowhere explicitly mentioned slavery. Douglass took this omission as a statement by the framers that the nation's future would have no room for slavery. Even in the face of hypocritical tolerance of slavery during celebrations of freedom and independence, he concluded, the core American document of political foundation—the Declaration of Independence—combined with his fellow citizens' changing attitudes to give him hope for the future.

One hundred eleven years after Douglass's oration, the Reverend Dr. Martin Luther King Jr. addressed a national audience. An organizer of the 1955 Montgomery, Alabama, bus boycott and a leader of the Southern Christian Leadership Conference, King helped to plan the March on Washington for Jobs and Freedom. On August 18, 1963, several hundred thousand demonstrators, white and black alike, marched through the nation's capital from the Washington Monument to the Lincoln Memorial. In the event's closing speech, Dr. King invoked the origins of the American republic:

> In a sense we've come to our nation's capital to cash a check. When the architects of our republic wrote the magnificent words of the Constitution and the Declaration of Independence, they were signing a promissory note to which every American was to fall heir. This note was a promise that all men, yes, black men as well as white men, would be guaranteed the "unalienable Rights" of "Life,

Liberty and the pursuit of Happiness." It is obvious today that America has defaulted on this promissory note, insofar as her citizens of color are concerned. Instead of honoring this sacred obligation, America has given the Negro people a bad check, a check which has come back marked "insufficient funds."

But we refuse to believe that the bank of justice is bankrupt. We refuse to believe that there are insufficient funds in the great vaults of opportunity of this nation. And so, we've come to cash this check, a check that will give us upon demand the riches of freedom and the security of justice.

Like Douglass, King pointed out that the founding fathers' words challenged America's failures; he urged African Americans to invoke the founding fathers' best aspirations as authority to confront and overcome the American experiment's failures.

On July 25, 1974, Representative Barbara Jordan (D-TX) followed in the rhetorical footsteps of Douglass and King. A first-term member of the House, Jordan brought to Congress a distinguished record of achievement as a Texas state senator. In the summer of 1974, as a member of the House Committee on the Judiciary, Jordan was one of those members of Congress who had to determine whether the alleged misdeeds of President Richard Nixon justified his impeachment. When she delivered her opening statement on the first day of the committee's hearings, Jordan invoked the Constitution's origins and the fraught relationship between it and African Americans:

Earlier today, we heard the beginning of the Preamble to the Constitution of the United States, "We, the people." It is a very eloquent beginning. But when the document was completed on the seventeenth of September 1787 I was not included in that "We, the people." I felt somehow for many years that George Washington and Alexander Hamilton just left me out by mistake. But through the process of amendment, interpretation and court decision I have finally been included in "We, the people."

Today, I am an inquisitor; I believe hyperbole would not be fictional and would not overstate the solemnness that I feel right now. My faith in the Constitution is whole, it is complete, it is total. I am not going to sit here and be an idle spectator to the diminution, the subversion, the destruction of the Constitution.

Yet again, Jordan sounded the central theme: despite the taint of slavery and racism, the principles at the Constitution's core, expanded and applied over the course of American history, were common property of all Americans; yet again, she challenged Americans to defend and vindicate those principles.

Thirteen years later, the nation commemorated the bicentennial of the framing of the US Constitution. Dissenting from the celebratory tone of the planned commemorations, Associate Justice Thurgood Marshall of the US Supreme Court delivered an address reprinted by law reviews across the nation. As lead counsel for the NAACP's Legal Defense Fund, Marshall had waged a

9. In 1974, Rep. Barbara Jordan (D-TX) argued that the legacies of the founding fathers demanded a searching inquiry into impeaching President Richard Nixon.

brilliant, hard-fought legal campaign against segregation and racial discrimination, battling to make the Thirteenth, Fourteenth, and Fifteenth Amendments legal realities rather than empty promises. In 1967, having served as a federal appellate judge in New York and then as solicitor-general of the United States, Marshall was appointed by President Lyndon B. Johnson as an associate justice of the Supreme Court, becoming the first African American justice.

In his 1987 address, Marshall challenged the bicentennial celebrations, focusing on the nature of the "more perfect Union" that the Constitution created. He protested the "complacent belief that the vision of those who debated and compromised in Philadelphia yielded the 'more perfect Union' it is said we now

**10. In 1987, Justice Thurgood Marshall challenged the bland and celebratory celebrations of the Constitution's bicentennial—and the founding fathers.**

enjoy." In measured rhetoric barely concealing his scorn, Marshall declined to share that "complacent belief":

> I do not believe that the meaning of the Constitution was forever "fixed" at the Philadelphia Convention. Nor do I find the wisdom, foresight, and sense of justice exhibited by the Framers particularly profound. To the contrary, the government they devised was defective from the start, requiring several amendments, a civil war, and momentous social transformation to attain the system of constitutional government, and its respect for the individual freedoms and human rights, we hold as fundamental today. When contemporary Americans cite "The Constitution," they invoke a concept that is vastly different from what the Framers barely began to construct two centuries ago.

Marshall diverged from Douglass's views while echoing King's and Jordan's arguments. He too insisted on "the evolving nature of the Constitution." Sketching the battles by which generations of Americans forced the nation to live up to the Constitution's promises, Marshall concluded:

> We will see that the true miracle was not the birth of the Constitution, but its life, a life nurtured through two turbulent centuries of our own making, and a life embodying much good fortune that was not.
>
> Thus, in this bicentennial year, we may not all participate in the festivities with flagwaving fervor. Some may more quietly commemorate the suffering, struggle, and sacrifice that has triumphed over much of what was wrong with the original document, and observe the anniversary with hopes not realized and promises not fulfilled. I plan to celebrate the bicentennial of the Constitution as a living document, including the Bill of Rights and the other amendments protecting individual freedoms and human rights.

Wearied by his service on the Court and his frustration with his colleagues' failure to understand the history he had endured and had helped to shape, Marshall was more dismissive of the founding fathers than Douglass, King, or Jordan had been—but he was equally committed to the power of the words they had shaped and the need to give those words real meaning.

On March 16, 2008, more than two decades after Justice Marshall's controversial lecture, Senator Barack Obama (D-IL) gave a speech at the Constitution Center in Philadelphia, Pennsylvania, on race's enduring significance in American history. Though the event was a critical juncture in his quest to become the Democratic nominee for president, Obama saw its larger significance, casting his oration as a principled reflection on issues of race and faith in American life.

Like his predecessors, Obama began with the Constitution's Preamble, the hopes of those who had framed it, their failings, and the ongoing struggle to repair those failings and bring constitutional realities in line with constitutional aspirations:

"We the people, in order to form a more perfect union."

Two hundred and twenty one years ago, in a hall that still stands across the street, a group of men gathered and, with these simple words, launched America's improbable experiment in democracy. Farmers and scholars; statesmen and patriots who had traveled across an ocean to escape tyranny and persecution finally made real their declaration of independence at a Philadelphia convention that lasted through the spring of 1787.

The document they produced was eventually signed but ultimately unfinished. It was stained by this nation's original sin of slavery, a question that divided the colonies and brought the convention to a stalemate until the founders chose to allow the slave trade to continue for at least twenty more years, and to leave any final resolution to future generations.

Of course, the answer to the slavery question was already embedded within our Constitution—a Constitution that had at its very core the ideal of equal citizenship under the law; a Constitution that promised its people liberty, and justice, and a union that could be and should be perfected over time.

And yet words on a parchment would not be enough to deliver slaves from bondage, or provide men and women of every color and creed their full rights and obligations as citizens of the United States. What would be needed were Americans in successive generations who were willing to do their part—through protests and struggle, on the streets and in the courts, through a civil war and civil disobedience and always at great risk—to narrow that gap between the promise of our ideals and the reality of their time.

Several months later, on the evening of November 4, 2008, Obama, the Democratic presidential nominee, achieved a decisive victory in the 2008 election. In his victory speech, the presumptive president, the first African American elected to the nation's highest office, acknowledged the history that he and his followers had made, linking it back to the founding fathers:

> If there is anyone out there who still doubts that America is a place where all things are possible, who still wonders if the dream of our Founders is alive in our time, who still questions the power of our democracy, tonight is your answer....
>
> And to all those who have wondered if America's beacon still burns as bright: tonight we proved once more that the true strength of our nation comes not from the might of our arms or the scale of our wealth, but from the enduring power of our ideals—democracy, liberty, opportunity and unyielding hope.
>
> That's the true genius of America that America can change. Our union can be perfected. And what we have already achieved gives us hope for what we can and must achieve tomorrow.

Following Obama's speech, commentators argued over whether his election fulfilled the founding fathers' dreams or whether any of them could have conceived his election as possible. The verdict of these discussions came close to the line of argument sketched in these pages—that Obama was invoking the best aspirations of the founding fathers and the efforts of later generations to narrow the gap between the ideals and the reality of the American experiment—to perfect the Union.

The theme remains constant. It echoes the words of a great work of religion and law that was centuries old when the founding fathers began their labors, the Talmud. As the Jewish sage Rabbi Tarfon counseled in *Ethics of the Fathers* (*Mishneh Pirke Avot* 2:21), "It is not thy duty to complete the work, but neither art thou free to desist from it."

# Chronology

| 1767–1770 | Colonial boycott of British goods |
| 1770 | Boston Massacre |
| | Adams defends British soldiers in Boston Massacre trials |
| | Parliament repeals Townshend Acts |
| 1773 | Parliament enacts Tea Act |
| | Radicals stage Boston Tea Party to dramatize opposition to Tea Act |
| 1774 | Parliament enacts "Intolerable Acts" |
| | Jefferson writes *A Summary View of the Rights of British America* |
| | First Continental Congress meets in Philadelphia |
| 1775 | Battles of Lexington and Concord |
| | Second Continental Congress convenes in Philadelphia |
| | Washington named commander in chief of Continental Army |
| | Congress submits Olive Branch Petition |
| | George III refuses to receive Olive Branch Petition |
| | George III proclaims colonies in rebellion |
| 1776 | Thomas Paine publishes *Common Sense* |
| | Adams publishes *Thoughts on Government* |
| | Congress authorizes framing of new state constitutions |
| | Congress declares American independence |
| | Congress edits, adopts Declaration of Independence drafted by Jefferson |
| | Washington withdraws from New York; British forces occupy the city |
| 1776–1777 | First wave of state constitution-making |
| 1777 | New York frames and adopts state constitution |
| | Battle of Saratoga |
| | Congress proposes Articles of Confederation to states |
| 1778 | Franklin negotiates alliance with France |
| 1779–1780 | Massachusetts frames and adopts state constitution |

| 1781 | Maryland's ratification puts Articles of Confederation into effect |
|------|------------------------------------------------------------------|
|      | Battle of Yorktown |
| 1782 | Adams negotiates treaty with Netherlands and loans to United States |
| 1782–1783 | Negotiations between Franklin, Adams, and Jay and British diplomats |
| 1783 | Treaty of Paris ends American War of Independence |
|      | Washington quells Newburgh Conspiracy |
|      | British evacuate occupied American states |
|      | Washington resigns as commander in chief |
| 1784 | Congress adopts Ordinance of 1784 |
| 1785 | Congress adopts Land Ordinance of 1785 |
|      | Mount Vernon Conference between Maryland and Virginia |
| 1786 | Annapolis Convention |
| 1787 | Federal Convention frames Constitution of the United States |
|      | Congress adopts Northwest Ordinance of 1787 |
| 1787–1788 | Ratification controversy; Constitution adopted by 11 of 13 states |
| 1788 | Confederation Congress declares Constitution adopted, arranges transition |
| 1789 | Washington unanimously elected first president of United States |
|      | First Congress creates executive departments of government |
|      | French Revolution begins with storming of Bastille |
|      | First Congress enacts Judiciary Act creating federal court system |
|      | First Congress proposes twelve constitutional amendments to states |
|      | North Carolina ratifies Constitution |
|      | Jay named first chief justice of the United States |

| 1790 | Treasury Secretary Hamilton submits *First Report on Public Credit* |
| | Franklin dies |
| | Rhode Island ratifies Constitution |
| | Hamilton submits *Second Report on Public Credit* |
| 1791 | Dispute within Washington's administration on bank bill's validity |
| | Hamilton submits *Report on Manufactures* |
| | Vermont becomes fourteenth state |
| | Virginia ratifies first ten amendments to Constitution (Bill of Rights) |
| 1792 | French depose King Louis XVI and declare First French Republic |
| | Kentucky becomes fifteenth state |
| | Washington unanimously reelected to presidency |
| 1792–1793 | Partisan conflict pits Federalists against Republicans |
| 1793 | French execute Louis XVI |
| | Washington issues Neutrality Proclamation |
| 1794 | Whiskey Rebellion is crushed by federal authorities |
| 1794–1795 | Chief Justice Jay negotiates treaty with Great Britain |
| 1795 | Jay Treaty with Great Britain intensifies partisan strife |
| | Jay, elected governor of New York, resigns as chief justice |
| 1796 | Washington announces retirement, publishes Farewell Address |
| | Adams elected second president of United States |
| 1797 | Adams sends diplomatic mission to France |
| 1798 | XYZ Affair |
| | Alien and Sedition Acts enacted |
| 1798–1799 | Quasi-war between France and the United States |
| 1799 | Washington dies |
| 1800 | Adams breaks with cabinet, sends peace mission to France |
| | Adams defeated in bid for second term as president |

# Appendix
# The founding fathers:
# A partial list

Nobody can agree on the complete list of the founding fathers, especially when we include Americans who did not hold political office. This list falls into three groups: (1) signers of the Declaration of Independence, (2) framers of the Constitution, and (3) those who were neither signers nor framers but who played pivotal roles in the creation of the United States.

## 1. Signers of the Declaration (by state delegation)

CONNECTICUT: Samuel Huntington, Roger Sherman, William Williams, Oliver Wolcott

DELAWARE: Thomas McKean, George Read, Caesar Rodney

GEORGIA: Button Gwinnett, Lyman Hall, George Walton

MARYLAND: Charles Carroll of Carrollton, Samuel Chase, William Paca, Thomas Stone

MASSACHUSETTS: John Adams, Samuel Adams, Elbridge Gerry, John Hancock, Robert Treat Paine

NEW HAMPSHIRE: Josiah Bartlett, Matthew Thornton, William Whipple

NEW JERSEY: Abraham Clark, John Hart, Francis Hopkinson, Richard Stockton, John Witherspoon

NEW YORK: William Floyd, Francis Lewis, Philip Livingston, Lewis Morris

NORTH CAROLINA: Joseph Hewes, William Hooper, John Penn

PENNSYLVANIA: George Clymer, Benjamin Franklin, Robert Morris, John Morton, George Ross, Benjamin Rush, James Smith, George Taylor, James Wilson

RHODE ISLAND: William Ellery, Stephen Hopkins

SOUTH CAROLINA: Thomas Heyward Jr., Thomas Lynch Jr., Arthur Middleton, Edward Rutledge

VIRGINIA: Carter Braxton, Benjamin Harrison, Thomas Jefferson, Francis Lightfoot Lee, Richard Henry Lee, Thomas Nelson Jr., George Wythe

## 2. Framers of the Constitution (by state delegations; asterisks denote signers)

CONNECTICUT: Oliver Ellsworth, William Samuel Johnson,* Roger Sherman*

DELAWARE: Richard Bassett,* Gunning Bedford Jr.,* Jacob Broome,* John Dickinson,* George Read*

GEORGIA: Abraham Baldwin,* William Few,* William Houstoun, William L. Pierce

MARYLAND: Daniel Carroll,* Daniel of St. Thomas Jenifer,* Luther Martin, James McHenry,* John Francis Mercer

MASSACHUSETTS: Elbridge Gerry, Nathaniel Gorham,* Rufus King,* Caleb Strong

NEW HAMPSHIRE: Nicholas Gilman,* John Langdon*

NEW JERSEY: David Brearly,* Jonathan Dayton,* William Churchill Houston, William Livingston,* William Paterson*

NEW YORK: Alexander Hamilton,* John Lansing Jr., Robert Yates

NORTH CAROLINA: William Blount,* William Richardson Davie, Alexander Martin, Richard Dobbs Spaight,* Hugh Williamson*

PENNSYLVANIA: George Clymer,* Thomas Fitzsimons,* Benjamin Franklin,* Jared Ingersoll,* Thomas Mifflin,* Gouverneur Morris,* Robert Morris,* James Wilson*

SOUTH CAROLINA: Pierce Butler,* Charles Pinckney,* Charles Cotesworth Pinckney,* John Rutledge*

VIRGINIA: John Blair,* James Madison Jr.,* George Mason, James McClurg, Edmund J. Randolph, George Washington,* George Wythe

## 3. Other founding fathers (and mothers)

Abigail Adams, wife of John Adams and mother of J. Q. Adams

John Quincy Adams, diplomat, US senator from Massachusetts, secretary of state, president of the United States, US representative from Massachusetts

Ethan Allen, war leader, founder of Vermont

Aaron Burr, war leader, US senator from New York, New York attorney-general, vice president of the United States

George Clinton, war leader, governor of New York, vice president of the United States

Patrick Henry, lawyer, Virginia legislator, governor of Virginia

James Iredell, attorney, North Carolina legislator, associate justice of US Supreme Court

John Jay, delegate to Continental Congress, president of Congress, diplomat, Confederation's secretary for Foreign Affairs, first chief justice of the United States, governor of New York

Henry Knox, war leader, secretary of war

Henry Laurens, South Carolina legislator, delegate to Continental Congress, diplomat

William Maclay, Pennsylvania legislator, US senator

John Marshall, diplomat, Virginia legislator, US representative and secretary of state, fourth chief justice of the United States

James Monroe, war leader, Virginia legislator, US senator, diplomat, governor of Virginia, secretary of war, secretary of state, president of the United States

Thomas Paine, pamphleteer

Mercy Otis Warren, author, pamphleteer, historian

# References

## Chapter 1: Words, images, meanings

For Harding's uses of "founding American fathers" and "founding fathers," see R. B. Bernstein, *The Founding Fathers Reconsidered* (New York: Oxford University Press, 2009), 1–2 and notes 1–2 to chapter 1.

"age of revolutions and constitutions" (Adams): John Adams to James Lloyd, 29 March 1815, in *The Works of John Adams*, ed. Charles Francis Adams, 10 vols. (Boston: Charles C. Little, and James Brown, 1850–56), 10:146–49 [quotation at 149]. (Hereafter Adams, *Works of Adams*).

"sense of continuity" (Dos Passos): John Dos Passos, *The Ground We Stand On: Some Examples from the History of a Political Creed* (New York: Harcourt, Brace, 1941), 3.

## Chapter 2: Contexts

For Franklin's 1766 testimony, see Carl Van Doren, *Benjamin Franklin* (New York: Viking Press, 1938), 336–55.

"remember the ladies": Abigail Adams to John Adams, 31 March to 5 April 1776 [electronic edition]. *Adams Family Papers: An Electronic Archive.* Massachusetts Historical Society. http://www.masshist.org/digitaladams/6.

"the blacks we rule over with such arbitrary sway": "From George Washington to Bryan Fairfax, 24 August 1774," Founders Online, National Archives (http://founders.archives.gov/documents/Washington/02-10-02-0097 [last update: 2014-12-01]). Source:

*The Papers of George Washington*, Colonial Series, Vol. 10: *21 March 1774–15 June 1775*, ed. W. W. Abbot and Dorothy Twohig (Charlottesville: University Press of Virginia, 1995), 154–56.

"drivers of negroes": Samuel Johnson, *Taxation No Tyranny . . .* (1775), in Samuel Johnson (Arthur Murphy, editor), *The Works of Samuel Johnson, LL.D., with an Essay on His Life and Genius* ("First Complete American Edition"), 2 vols. (New-York: Alexander V. Blake, 1843), 2: 429–38 [quotation at 437 col. 2].

"cautiously transforming egalitarianism": Richard B. Morris, *The Forging of the Union, 1781–1789* (New York: Harper & Row, 1987), at 162–93.

"in all cases whatsoever": Declaratory Act of 1766, 6 Geo. III c.12, at http://teachingamericanhistory.org/library/document/the-declaratory-act/.

"the old good nature": John Adams to John Jay, 2 June 1785, in Adams, *Works of Adams*, 8:255–59.

"Let us dare . . .": John Adams, *A Dissertation on the Canon and Feudal Law* (1765), in *The Revolutionary Writings of John Adams*, C. Bradley Thompson (Indianapolis, IN: Liberty Fund, 2000), 21–35 [quotation at 32–33].

Pope epitaph for Newton: Alexander Pope, "Epitaph Intended for Sir Isaac Newton, in Westminster Abbey" (written and published 1730), in Alexander Pope (John Butt, editor), *The Poems of Alexander Pope: A Reduced Version of the Twickenham Text* (New Haven, CT: Yale University Press, 1963), 808.

"empire of reason": Noah Webster, *An Examination into the Leading Principles of the Federal Constitution* (Philadelphia, PA: Prichard and Hall, 1787), 6.

## Chapter 3: Achievements and challenges

"the experiment of an extended republic": James Madison, *The Federalist* No. 14, in Alexander Hamilton, James Madison, and John Jay (Jacob E. Cooke, editor), *The Federalist* (Middletown, CT: Wesleyan University Press, 1961), 83–99 [quotation at 88]. Hereafter Hamilton, Madison, and Jay, *The Federalist*.

"capable or not": Alexander Hamilton, *The Federalist* No. 1, in Hamilton, Madison, and Jay, *The Federalist*, 3–7 [quotation at 3].

"May it be to the world": "From Thomas Jefferson to Roger Chew Weightman, 24 June 1826," Founders Online, National Archives (http://founders.archives.gov/documents/Jefferson/98-01-02-6179

[last update: 2014-12-01]). Source: this is an Early Access document from *The Papers of Thomas Jefferson: Retirement Series.*

"political building": Benjamin Franklin, speech in Convention, 28 June 1787, in *The Records of the Federal Convention of 1787*, ed. Max Farrand, 4 vols. (New Haven, CT: Yale University Press, 1911, 1937, 1966, 1987), 1:450–52 [quotation at 451]. Hereafter Farrand, *Records.*

"putt Men upon Thinking"; John Adams to James Warren, 11 April 1776, in Robert J. Taylor et al., eds., *The Papers of John Adams*, 3d series, 15 vols. to date (Cambridge, MA: Belknap Press of Harvard University Press, 1977–), 4:132.

"tedious, intricate, and expensive": George Mason, "Objections to the Constitution of the United States. . ." [October 1787], http://teachingamericanhistory.org/library/document/objections-to-the-constitution/.

"a federal republic": James Wilson, "State House Speech," October 6, 1787, in John Bach McMaster and Frederick D. Stone, eds., *Pennsylvania and the Federal Constitution, 1787–1788.* (Lancaster: Published for the Subscribers by the Historical Society of Pennsylvania, 1888), 143–44.

"a NATION without a NATIONAL GOVERNMENT": Alexander Hamilton, *The Federalist* No. 85, in Hamilton, Madison, and Jay, *The Federalist*, 587–95 [quotation at 594–95].

"I am captivated": "From Thomas Jefferson to James Madison, 20 December 1787," Founders Online, National Archives (http://founders.archives.gov/documents/Jefferson/01-12-02-0454 [last update: 2014-12-01]). Source: *The Papers of Thomas Jefferson*, Vol. 12: *7 August 1787–31 March 1788*, ed. Julian P. Boyd (Princeton, NJ: Princeton University Press, 1955), 438–43.

"happy talent": John Adams to Timothy Pickering, 6 August 1822, in Adams, *Works of Adams*, 2:154.

"definitions and axioms": Abraham Lincoln to Henry L. Pierce and others, 6 April 1859, in *Collected Works of Abraham Lincoln*, ed. Roy P. Basler, 9 vols. (New Brunswick, NJ: Rutgers University Press, 1953–1955), 3:374–76 [quotation at 375]. Hereafter Basler, *CWAL.*

"three volumes bound in marbled paper": Thomas Jefferson, "Anas: Explanation of the three volumes bound in marbled paper," in Thomas Jefferson, *Memoirs, Correspondence, and Miscellanies from the Papers of Thomas Jefferson* (Thomas Jefferson Randolph, editor) (Charlottesville, VA: F. Carr and Co., 1829), 3:443.

"splendid misery": "From Thomas Jefferson to Elbridge Gerry, 13 May 1797," Founders Online, National Archives (http://founders. archives.gov/documents/Jefferson/01-29-02-0288 [last update: 2014-12-01]). Source: *The Papers of Thomas Jefferson,* Vol. 29: *1 March 1796–31 December 1797,* ed. Barbara B. Oberg (Princeton, NJ: Princeton University Press, 2002), 361–66.

"Memorial and Remonstrance": "Memorial and Remonstrance against Religious Assessments, [ca. 20 June] 1785," Founders Online, National Archives (http://founders.archives.gov/documents/ Madison/01-08-02-0163 [last update: 2014-12-01]). Source: *The Papers of James Madison,* Vol. 8: *10 March 1784–28 March 1786,* ed. Robert A. Rutland and William M. E. Rachal (Chicago: University of Chicago Press, 1973), 295–306.

"All men are created equal": "V. The Declaration of Independence as Adopted by Congress, 11 June–4 July 1776," Founders Online, National Archives (http://founders.archives.gov/documents/ Jefferson/01-01-02-0176-0006 [last update: 2014-12-01]). Source: *The Papers of Thomas Jefferson,* Vol. 1: *1760–1776,* ed. Julian P. Boyd (Princeton, NJ: Princeton University Press, 1950), 429–33.

"as to Slaves" (Gerry): James Madison, notes of debates on August 22, 1787, in Farrand, *Records,* 2:369–77 [quotation at 372].

"invitation to struggle": Edward S. Corwin, *The President: Office and Powers, 1787–1957: Analysis of Practice and Opinion,* 4th ed. (New York: New York University Press, 1957), 171.

"decision, activity, secrecy, and dispatch": Alexander Hamilton, *The Federalist* No. 70, in Hamilton, Madison, and Jay, *The Federalist,* 471–80 [quotation at 472].

"a wisdom more than human": Thomas Jefferson to Samuel Kercheval, 13 July 1816, at Jefferson, Thomas, 1743–1826. Letters, Electronic Text Center, University of Virginia Library, online at http://etext. virginia.edu/etcbin/toccer-new2?id=JefLett.sgm&images=images/ modeng&data=/texts/english/modeng/parsed&tag=public&part=2 44&division=div1.

"Our Country, my Friend, is not yet out of Danger": John Adams to Samuel Adams, 1 May 1784, Samuel Adams Papers, Bancroft Collection, Rare Books and Manuscripts Division, New York Public Library, Astor, Lenox, and Tilden Foundations.

"on the Necks of the Senate": William Maclay, entry for 22 August 1789, in *The Diary of William Maclay and Other Notes on Senate Debates, March 4, 1789–March 3, 1791,* vol. 9 of *The Documentary History of the First Federal Congress...,* ed. Kenneth R. Bowling and Heen E. Veit (Baltimore, MD: Johns Hopkins University Press, 1988), 128–31 [quotations at 130].

"Posterity!": John Adams to Abigail Adams, 26 April 1777 [electronic edition]. *Adams Family Papers: An Electronic Archive.* Massachusetts Historical Society. http://www.masshist.org/digitaladams/.

## Chapter 4: Legacies

"joint and very unanimous councils": John Jay, *The Federalist* No. 2, in Hamilton, Madison, and Jay, *The Federalist*, 8–13 [quote at 10–11].

"I revere these illustrious personages": Luther Martin, *The Genuine Information . . .* , in Farrand, *Records*, item clviii, paragraph 9.

"the father of his country": Henry Lee, "The Father of His Country," in *The World's Great Orators and Their Best Orations*, ed. Charles Morris (Philadelphia, PA: John C. Winston Co., 1902), 47–52 [quotation at 47].

"once hardy . . . race of ancestors": Abraham Lincoln, "Address before the Young Men's Lyceum of Springfield, Illinois," 27 January 1838, in Basler, *CWAL*, 1:108–15.

"Our age is retrospective": Ralph Waldo Emerson, *Nature* (orig. ed. 1836), reprinted in Ralph Waldo Emerson, *Essays and Lectures*, ed. Joel Porte (New York: Library of America, 1983), 5:5–49 [quotation at 7].

"a new nation, conceived in liberty:" Abraham Lincoln, "Address Delivered at the Dedication of the Cemetery at Gettysburg," [Gettysburg Address], 19 November 1863, in Basler, *CWAL*, 7:17–23.

"a machine that would go of itself": James Russell Lowell, "The Place of the Independent in Politics: An Address Delivered before the Reform Club of New York, at Steinway Hall, April 13, 1888," in James Russell Lowell, *Literary and Political Addresses* (Boston, MA: Houghton, Mifflin, 1891), 190–221 [quotation at 206].

"Founders Chic": Evan Thomas, "Founders Chic: Live from Philadelphia," *Newsweek*, 9 July 2001, at 48–49.

"Abraham Lincoln was no superman": Warren G. Harding, "Address on the Dedication of the Lincoln Memorial," *New York Times*, 31 May 1922, at 1, 3 [quotation at 3].

"our fathers, who framed the government under which we live": Abraham Lincoln, "Address at Cooper Institute, New York City," 27 February 1860, in Basler, *CWAL*, 522–50 [quotation at 535].

## Epilogue

For the text of Frederick Douglass's 1852 speech, I have used Ted Widmer, ed., *American Speeches: Political Oratory from the Revolution to the Civil War* (New York: Library of America, 2006), 526–52.

For the text of Reverend Dr. Martin Luther King Jr.'s 1963 speech, I have used Ted Widmer, ed., *American Speeches: Political Oratory from Abraham Lincoln to Bill Clinton* (New York: Library of America, 2006), 556–73.

For the text of Barbara Jordan's 1974 speech, I have used Widmer, ed., *American Speeches: Lincoln to Clinton*, 695–99.

For the text of Thurgood Marshall's 1987 address, originally delivered at the annual seminar of the San Francisco Patent and Trademark Law Association in Maui, Hawaii, on 6 May 1987, I have used the version published as Thurgood Marshall, "Commentary: Reflections on the Bicentennial of the United States Constitution," *Harvard Law Review* 101:1 (November 1987): 1–5. See also Charles L. Zelden, *Thurgood Marshall: Race, Rights, and the Struggle for a More Perfect Union* (London: Routledge, 2013), 192–96.

For Barack Obama's Constitution Center 2008 speech, I have used "Barack Obama's Speech on Race," *New York Times*, 19 March 2008, online at www.nytimes.com/2008/03/18/us/politics/18text-obama.html?_r=1& ref=politics&oref=slogin (viewed online 5 October 2008).

For Barack Obama's victory statement on Election Day 2008, I have used "Transcript: Obama's Victory Speech," *New York Times*, 5 November 2008, online at www.nytimes.com/2008/11/04/us/politics/04text-obama.html? pagewanted=1&sq= november%204%202008%20obama%20speech&st= cse&scp=1 (viewed online 30 November 2008).

For the quotation from the Talmud, see *Sayings of the Fathers: Pirke Aboth: The Hebrew Text, with English Translation and Commentary by Rabbi Joseph H. Hertz* (West Orange, NJ: Behrman House, 1986), at 45.

# Further reading

Readers seeking further documentation and elaboration of the arguments made in this book should see R. B. Bernstein, *The Founding Fathers Reconsidered* (New York: Oxford University Press, 2009), and Richard B. Bernstein with Kym S. Rice, *Are We to Be a Nation? The Making of the Constitution* (Cambridge, MA: Harvard University Press, 1987).

Understanding the founding fathers begins with reading their own words. The Library of America has issued volumes for many of the key figures and events examined here: Gordon S. Wood, ed., *John Adams: Revolutionary Writings, 1755–1775* and *1775–1783*, 2 vols. (New York: Library of America, 2011) (two further volumes projected); J. A. Leo LeMay, ed., *Benjamin Franklin: Writings* (New York: Library of America, 1987); Joanne B. Freeman, ed., *Alexander Hamilton: Writings* (New York: Library of America, 2001); Merrill D. Peterson, ed., *Thomas Jefferson: Writings* (New York: Library of America, 1984); Jack N. Rakove, ed., *James Madison: Writings* (New York: Library of America, 1999); Charles F. Hobson, ed., *John Marshall: Writings* (New York: Library of America, 2010); Eric Foner, ed., *Thomas Paine: Collected Writings* (New York: Library of America, 1995); John H. Rhodehamel, ed., *George Washington: Writings* (New York: Library of America, 1997); Bernard Bailyn, ed., *The Debate on the Constitution*, 2 vols. (New York: Library of America, 1993); and John H. Rhodehamel, ed., *The American Revolution: Writings from the War of Independence* (New York: Library of America, 2001). Edith Gelles is now editing a volume for Abigail Adams.

In a class by itself is John P. Kaminski, ed., *The Founders on the Founders: Word Portraits from the American Revolutionary Era* (Charlottesville: University of Virginia Press, 2008).

The best one-volume history of the American Revolution is Robert Middlekauff, *The Glorious Cause: The American Revolution, 1763–1789* (New York: Oxford University Press, 1982; revised edition, 2005). Two books by John E. Ferling complement Middlekauff's account—*Almost a Miracle: The American Victory in the War for Independence* (New York: Oxford University Press, 2007) and *A Leap in the Dark: The Struggle to Create the American Republic* (New York: Oxford University Press, 2003). See also Bernard Bailyn, *The Ideological Origins of the American Revolution* (Cambridge, MA: Belknap Press of Oxford University Press, 1967; expanded ed., 1992); Andrew J. O'Shaughnessy, *The Man Who Lost America: British Leadership, the American Revolution, and the Fall of the Empire* (New Haven, CT: Yale University Press, 2013). Richard B. Morris, *The Forging of the Union, 1781–1789* (New York; Harper & Row, 1987), the premier history of the United States during the Confederation period, deserves to be restored to print; readers will also find valuable Merrill M. Jensen, *The Articles of Confederation: An Interpretation of the Social-Constitutional History of the American Revolution* (Madison: University of Wisconsin Press, 1948; reprint, 1970); Jensen, *The New Nation: A History of the United States during the Confederation, 1781–1789* (New York: Alfred A. Knopf, 1950; reprint, Boston, MA: Northeastern University Press, 1981); Jensen, *The Founding of a Nation: A History of the American Revolution, 1763–1776* (New York: Oxford University Press, 1968; reprint, Indianapolis, IN: Hackett, 2004); and Jensen, *The American Revolution within America* (New York: New York University Press, 1974). Three other books by Richard B. Morris are recommended: *The American Revolution Reconsidered* (New York: Harper & Row, 1967); *The Emerging Nations and the American Revolution* (New York: Harper & Row, 1970); and *Seven Who Shaped Our Destiny: The Founding Fathers as Revolutionaries* (New York: Harper & Row, 1973). Jack N. Rakove, *The Beginnings of National Politics: An Interpretive History of the Continental Congress* (New York: Alfred A. Knopf, 1999), and *Original Meanings: Politics and Ideas in the Making of the Constitution* (New York: Alfred A. Knopf, 1996) are indispensable, as are Richard R. Beeman, Stephen Botein, and Edward C. Carter II, eds., *Beyond Confederation: Dimensions of the Constitution and*

*American National Identity* (Chapel Hill: University of North Carolina Press for the Institute of Early American History and Culture, 1987), and the four studies by Pauline Maier: *From Resistance to Revolution: Colonial Radicals and the Development of American Opposition to Britain, 1765-1776* (New York: Alfred A. Knopf, 1972; paperback reprint, New York: W. W. Norton, 1991); *The Old Revolutionaries: Political Lives in the Age of Samuel Adams* (New York: Alfred A. Knopf, 1980; paperback reprint, New York: W. W. Norton, 1991); *American Scripture: Making the Declaration of Independence* (New York: Alfred A. Knopf, 1997); and *Ratification: The People Debate the Constitution, 1787-1788* (New York: Simon & Schuster, 2009). See also Gordon S. Wood, *The Creation of the American Republic, 1776-1787* (Chapel Hill: University of North Carolina Press for the Institute of Early American History and Culture, 1969; new edition, 1996); Willi Paul Adams (Rita and Robert Kimber, trans.), *The First American Constitutions*, expanded ed. (Lanham, MD: Madison House/Rowman and Littlefield, 2000 [orig. ed. 1980]), Jurgen O. Heideking, *The Constitution before the Judgment Seat: The Prehistory and Ratification of the American Constitution, 1787-1791* (Charlottesville: University of Virginia Press, 2012); and the many works of Edmund S. Morgan.

For international background and context, see R. R. Palmer, *The Age of the Democratic Revolution: A Political History of Europe and America, 1760-1800* (Princeton, NJ: Princeton University Press, 1959, 1964; one-vol. ed., 2014), and William Doyle, *Aristocracy and Its Enemies in the Age of Revolution* (Oxford: Oxford University Press, 2009).

On the American Enlightenment, see Henry Steele Commager, *Empire of Reason: How Europe Imagined and America Realized the Enlightenment* (New York: Anchor Press/Doubleday, 1977); Commager, *Jefferson, Nationalism, and the Enlightenment* (New York: George Braziller, 1975); Douglass G. Adair (Trevor Colbourn, ed.), *Fame and the Founding Fathers: Essays of Douglass Adair* (New York: W. W. Norton for the Institute of Early American History and Culture, 1974; reprint, Indianapolis, IN: Liberty Fund, 1998); Henry F. May, *The Enlightenment in America* (New York: Oxford University Press, 1976); I. Bernard Cohen, *Science and the Founding Fathers; Science in the Political Thought of Jefferson, Adams, Franklin, and Madison* (New York: W. W. Norton, 1995; revised paperback ed., 1997); and Robert A. Ferguson, *The American*

*Enlightenment, 1750–1820* (Cambridge, MA: Harvard University Press, 1997). Two other books by Ferguson are especially illuminating on the difficulty of ordering the world with words: *Law and Letters in American Culture* (Cambridge, MA: Harvard University Press, 1984) and *Reading the Early Republic* (Cambridge, MA: Harvard University Press, 2004).

On the framing of the Constitution, see Clinton L. Rossiter, *1787: The Grand Convention* (New York: Macmillan, 1966); Richard R. Beeman, *Plain, Honest Men: The Making of the American Constitution* (New York: Random House, 2009); Carol Berkin, *A Brilliant Solution: Inventing the American Constitution* (New York: Harcourt, 2002); Max Farrand, *The Framing of the Constitution of the United States* (New Haven, CT: Yale University Press, 1913); and Charles Warren, *The Making of the Constitution* (Boston: Little, Brown, 1926, 1937). The peerless compilation of primary documents is Max Farrand, ed., *The Records of the Federal Convention of 1787*, 4 vols. (1987 supplement edited by James H. Hutson) (New Haven, CT: Yale University Press, 1911, 1937, 1966, 1987). On putting it into effect, see Leonard D. White, *The Federalists: A Study in Administrative History, 1789–1801* (New York: Macmillan, 1948), and Frank D. Bourgin, *The Great Challenge: The Myth of Laissez-Faire in the Early Republic* (corrected ed., New York: Harper & Row, 1990).

On the political history of the early republic see Joanne B. Freeman, *Affairs of Honor: National Politics in the New Republic* (New Haven, CT: Yale University Press, 2001); Gordon S. Wood, *Empire of Liberty: A History of the Early Republic, 1789–1815* (New York: Oxford University Press, 2009); Francis D. Cogliano, *Revolutionary America, 1763–1815: A Political History* (London: Routledge, 1999; second edition, 2009); and Paul E. Johnson, *The Early American Republic, 1789–1829* (New York: Oxford University Press, 2007).

On individual founding fathers see Edmund S. Morgan, *Benjamin Franklin* (New Haven, CT: Yale University Press, 2002); Gordon S. Wood, *The Americanization of Benjamin Franklin* (New York: Penguin Press, 2004); Esmond Wright, *Franklin of Philadelphia* (Cambridge, MA: Harvard University Press, 1986); Marcus Cunliffe, *George Washington: Man and Monument* (Boston: Little, Brown, 1958, and many reprints); Glenn A. Phelps, *George Washington and American Constitutionalism* (Lawrence: University Press of Kansas,

1993); Robert F. Jones, *George Washington: Ordinary Man, Extraordinary Leader* (New York: Fordham University Press, 2002); Ron Chernow, *Washington* (New York: Penguin Press, 2010); John Rhodehamel, *The Great Experiment: George Washington and the American Republic* (New Haven, CT: Yale University Press, 1999); James Grant, *John Adams: Party of One* (New York: Farrar, Straus and Giroux, 2005); Zoltan Haraszti, *John Adams and the Prophets of Progress* (Cambridge, MA: Harvard University Press, 1952); C. Bradley Thompson, *John Adams and the Spirit of Liberty* (Lawrence: University Press of Kansas, 1998); Peter Shaw, *The Character of John Adams* (Chapel Hill: University of North Carolina Press for the Institute of Early American History and Culture, 1975); Joseph J. Ellis, *Passionate Sage: The Character and Legacy of John Adams* (New York: W. W. Norton, 1993); Gilbert Chinard, *Honest John Adams* (Boston, MA: Little, Brown, 1935); R. B. Bernstein, *The Education of John Adams* (New York: Oxford University Press, forthcoming, 2016); Edith B. Gelles, *Portia: The World of Abigail Adams* (Bloomington: Indiana University Press, 1992); Gelles, *First Thoughts: Life and Letters of Abigail Adams* (New York: Twayne, 1998), reprinted in paperback as *Abigail Adams: A Writing Life* (London: Routledge, 2002); Gelles, *Abigail and John: Portrait of a Marriage* (New York: William Morrow, 2009); Woody Holton, *Abigail Adams: A Life* (New York: Free Press, 2009); R. B. Bernstein, *Thomas Jefferson* (New York: Oxford University Press, 2003); Merrill D. Peterson, *Thomas Jefferson and the New Nation* (New York: Oxford University Press, 1971); Peter S. Onuf, ed., *Jeffersonian Legacies* (Charlottesville: University Press of Virginia, 1993); Onuf, *Jefferson's Empire: The Language of American Nationhood* (Charlottesville: University Press of Virginia, 2000); Onuf, *The Mind of Thomas Jefferson* (Charlottesville: University Press of Virginia, 2007); Kevin P. Hayes, *The Road to Monticello: The Life and Mind of Thomas Jefferson* (New York: Oxford University Press, 2008); Jeremy D. Bailey, *Thomas Jefferson and Executive Power* (Cambridge: Cambridge University Press, 2007); Hannah Spahn, *Thomas Jefferson, Time, and History* (Charlottesville: University of Virginia Press, 2011); Brian Steele, *Thomas Jefferson and American Nationhood* (Cambridge: Cambridge University Press, 2012); Francis D. Cogliano, *Emperor of Liberty: Thomas Jefferson's Foreign Policy* (New Haven, CT: Yale University Press, 2014); Ralph Ketcham, *James Madison* (New York: Macmillan, 1971; reprint, Charlottesville: University Press of Virginia, 1998); Jack N. Rakove, *James Madison* and the Creation of the American Republic, 3rd ed. (New York: Pearson/Longman, 2007); Forrest McDonald, *Alexander Hamilton* (New York: W. W. Norton, 1979); Ron Chernow, *Alexander Hamilton* (New York: Penguin Press, 2004); Gerald Stourzh, *Alexander Hamilton and the Idea of Republican Government* (Stanford, CA: Stanford University Press, 1970); Forrest McDonald, *Alexander Hamilton* (New York: W. W. Norton, 1979); Karl-Friedrich Walling, *Republican Empire: Alexander Hamilton on War and Free Government* (Lawrence: University Press of Kansas, 1999); John Lamberton Harper, *American Machiavelli: Alexander Hamilton and the Origins of U.S. Foreign Policy* (Cambridge: Cambridge University Press, 2005); Clinton Rossiter, *Alexander Hamilton and the Constitution* (New York: Harcourt, Brace & World, 1964); Richard B. Morris, *John Jay, the Nation, and the Court* (Boston: Boston University Press, 1967); Walter Stahr, *John Jay: Founding Father* (New York: Hambledon and London, 2005). See also Mark David Hall, *Roger Sherman and the Creation of the American Republic* (New York: Oxford University Press, 2013); Jane E. Calvert, *Quaker Constitutionalism and the Political Thought of John Dickinson* (Cambridge: Cambridge University Press, 2009); Eric S. Foner, *Tom Paine and Revolutionary America* (New York: Oxford University Press, 1976; new ed., 2004); R. Kent Newmyer, *John Marshall and the Heroic Age of the Supreme Court* (Baton Rouge: Louisiana State University Press, 2001); George Athan Billias, *Elbridge Gerry: Founding Father and Republican Statesman* (New York: McGraw-Hill, 1976); J. Kent McGaughey, *Richard Henry Lee of Virginia: A Portrait of an American Revolutionary* (Lanham, MD: Rowman and Littlefield, 2003); and Alfred F. Young, *The Shoemaker and the Tea Party: Memory and the American Revolution* (Boston, MA: Beacon Press, 1999).

On what history has made of the founding fathers, see Wesley Frank Craven, *The Legend of the Founding Fathers* (New York: New York University Press, 1957); Michael G. Kammen, *A Season of Youth: The American Revolution and the Historical Imagination* (New York: Knopf, 1978); Kammen, *A Machine That Would Go of Itself: The Constitution and American Culture* (New York: Alfred A. Knopf, 1986, and reprint editions); Kammen, *Mystic Chords of Memory: The Transformation of Tradition in American Culture* (New York: Alfred A. Knopf, 1991); and Karal Ann Marling, *George Washington Slept Here: Colonial Revivals and American Culture, 1876–1986*

(Cambridge, MA: Harvard University Press, 1988). Two books by David Lowenthal posit the distinction between "history" and "heritage" at the core of current debates: *The Past Is a Foreign Country* (Cambridge: Cambridge University Press, 1986), and *Possessed by the Past: The Heritage Crusade and the Spoils of History* (New York: Free Press, 1996), reprinted in paperback as *The Heritage Crusade and the Spoils of History* (Cambridge: Cambridge University Press, 1998).

On the reputations of individual founding fathers, see Merrill D. Peterson, *The Jefferson Image in the American Mind* (New York: Oxford University Press, 1960; reprint, with new foreword, Charlottesville: University Press of Virginia, 1998); Francis D. Cogliano, *Thomas Jefferson: Reputation and Legacy* (Charlottesville: University of Virginia Press, 2006); Annette Gordon-Reed, *Thomas Jefferson and Sally Hemings: An American Controversy* (Charlottesville: University Press of Virginia, 1997; reprint with new introduction, 1999); Jan Ellen Lewis and Peter S. Onuf, eds., *Sally Hemings and Thomas Jefferson: History, Memory, and Civic Culture* (Charlottesville: University Press of Virginia, 1999); Annette Gordon-Reed, *The Hemingses of Monticello: An American Family* (New York: W. W. Norton, 2008); Peter S. Onuf, ed., *Jeffersonian Legacies* (Charlottesville: University Press of Virginia, 1993); Stephen Knott, *Alexander Hamilton and the Persistence of Myth* (Lawrence: University Press of Kansas, 2002); Nian-sheng Huang, *Benjamin Franklin in American Thought and Culture, 1790–1990* (Philadelphia: American Philosophical Society, 1994); Barry Schwartz, *George Washington: The Making of an American Symbol* (New York: Free Press/Macmillan, 1987).

On slavery, see Paul Finkelman, *Slavery and the Founders: Race and Liberty in the Age of Jefferson*, 3rd ed. (London: Routledge, 2014); Donald L. Robinson, *Slavery and the Structure of American Politics, 1765–1820* (New York: Harcourt Brace Jovanovich, 1971); A. Leon Higginbotham, *In the Matter of Color: Race and the American Legal Process: The Colonial Period* (New York: Oxford University Press, 1978); and Winthrop D. Jordan, *White over Black: American Attitudes toward the Negro, 1550–1812* (Chapel Hill: University of North Carolina Press for Institute of Early American History and Culture, 1968; new ed., 2012). The many works of David Brion Davis are indispensable.

On women, see Linda K. Kerber, *Women of the Republic: Intellect and Ideology in Revolutionary America* (Chapel Hill: University of North Carolina Press for the Institute of Early American History and Culture, 1980); Carol Berkin, *Revolutionary Mothers: Women in the Struggle for American Independence* (New York: Knopf, 2005); and Rosemarie Zagarri, *Revolutionary Backlash: Women and Politics in the Early American Republic* (Philadelphia: University of Pennsylvania Press, 2007).

On law, see William E. Nelson, *The Common Law in Colonial America*, 2 vols. of 4 projected (New York: Oxford University Press, 2008, 2012); William E. Nelson, *Americanization of the Common Law: The Impact of Legal Change on Massachusetts Society, 1760–1830* (Cambridge, MA: Harvard University Press, 1975; new ed., Athens: University of Georgia Press, 1994); R. Kent Newmyer, *The Supreme Court under Marshall and Taney*, 2nd ed. (Wheeling, IL: Harlan Davidson, 2006); Charles F. Hobson, *The Great Chief Justice: John Marshall and the Rule of Law* (Lawrence: University Press of Kansas, 1996); Maeva Marcus, ed., *Origins of the Federal Judiciary: Essays on the Judiciary Act of 1789* (New York: Oxford University Press, 1992); Mary Sarah Bilder, Maeva Marcus, and R. Kent Newmyer, eds., *Blackstone in America: Essays of Kathryn Preyer* (Cambridge: Cambridge University Press, 2009) (far more wide-ranging than its title suggests); and the many studies of John Phillip Reid, especially *Constitutional History of the American Revolution*, 4 vols. (Madison: University of Wisconsin Press, 1986–1993; one-vol. abr. ed., 1995).

On religion, see David F. Holmes, *The Faiths of the Founding Fathers* (New York: Oxford University Press, 2008); Edwin S. Gaustad, *Faith of the Founders: Religion and the New Nation, 1776–1826* (Waco, TX: Baylor University Press, 2004); Patricia U. Bonomi, *Under the Cope of Heaven: Religion, Society, and Politics in Colonial America*, updated ed. (New York: Oxford University Press, 2003; orig. ed., 1986); and Thomas J. Curry, *Separation of Church and State to the Passage of the First Amendment* (New York: Oxford University Press, 1986).

On originalism, see Edward A. Purcell Jr., *Originalism, Federalism, and the American Constitutional Experience: A Historical Inquiry* (New Haven, CT: Yale University Press, 2007); Gerhard Casper, *Separating Power: Essays from the Founding Period* (Cambridge, MA:

Harvard University Press, 1997); Leonard W. Levy, *Original Intent and the Framers' Constitution* (New York: Macmillan, 1987); Jack N. Rakove, ed., *Interpreting the Constitution: The Debate over Original Intent* (Boston: Northeastern University Press, 1990); Joseph M. Lynch, *Negotiating the Constitution: The Earliest Debates over Original Intent* (Ithaca, NY: Cornell University Press, 1999); Jonathan O'Neill, *Originalism in American Law and Politics: A Constitutional History* (Baltimore: Johns Hopkins University Press, 2005); Dennis J. Goldford, *The American Constitution and the Debate over Originalism* (Cambridge: Cambridge University Press, 2005); Alan Gibson, *Interpreting the Founding: Guide to the Enduring Debates over the Origins and Foundations of the American Republic* (Lawrence: University Press of Kansas, 2006, 2nd ed. 2010); Alan Gibson, *Understanding the Founding: The Crucial Questions* (Lawrence: University Press of Kansas, 2007, 2nd ed. 2010). See also, for an innovative and challenging critique, Martin S. Flaherty, "History 'Lite' in Modern American Constitutionalism," *Columbia Law Review* 95 (1995): 523–90.

The McConnell Center at the University of Louisville sponsored a research project to identify forgotten founding fathers. In 2008, the Center published the first edition of its report, Gary L. Gregg II and Mark David Hall, eds., *America's Forgotten Founders* (Louisville, KY: Butler Books, 2008; 2nd ed., Wilmington, DE: Intercollegiate Studies Institute, 2011), identifying the top ten forgotten founders as James Wilson, George Mason, Gouverneur Morris, John Jay, Roger Sherman, John Marshall, John Dickinson, Thomas Paine, Patrick Henry, and John Witherspoon. The book blends historical rediscovery and reflections on the cultural and political significance of the founding fathers. For an interesting counterweight, see Alfred F. Young, Gary B. Nash, and Ray Raphael, eds., *Revolutionary Founders: Rebels, Radicals, and Reformers in the Making of the Nation* (New York: Alfred A. Knopf, 2011); Ray Raphael, *Founders: The People Who Brought You a Nation* (New York: New Press, 2009); Raphael, *The First American Revolution: Before Lexington and Concord* (New York: New Press, 2002); and Raphael, *A People's History of the American Revolution: How Common People Shaped Our Fight for Independence* (New York: New Press, 2001).

# Index

(Pages denoting figures are followed by an italicized *f*.)